*The*

# INVITATION

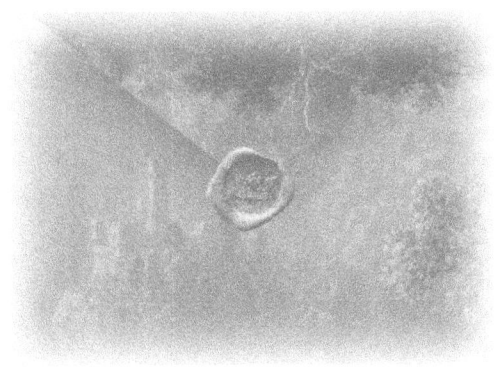

*Discover Kingdom Identity and Purpose*

## K. LEE BROWN

Copyright © 2025 K. Lee Brown All rights reserved.

No part of this publication may be reproduced, stored, or transmitted in any form or by any means, including written, copied, or electronically, without prior written permission from the author or his agents. The only exception is brief quotations in printed reviews. Short excerpts may be used with the publisher's or author's expressed written permission.

All Scripture quotations, unless otherwise noted, are from the Berean Standard Version of the Bible.

The Invitation: Discover Kingdom Identity and Purpose

Cover and Interior Page design by True Potential, Inc.

ISBN: (Paperback): 9781960024794

ISBN: (e-book): 9781960024800

LCCN: 9781960024794

True Potential, Inc.
PO Box 904, Travelers Rest, SC 29690
www.truepotentialmedia.com
Cover and Interior Page design by True Potential, Inc.

*"I've had the privilege of knowing Lee for years, and his brilliance in both psychology and theology shines through in The Invitation. This book is more than just a theological exploration—it's a transformative call to reclaim your identity as God's cherished inheritance."* - **Kilton Janvier, Pastor, Next Gen Specialist, Content Creator**

*"I believe this book will inspire, challenge and empower you to accept the Masters Invitation to fully, completely and without reservations, Follow Him into your destiny!!*
- **Pastor Lonnie Johns, Lead Pastor Christ Central Church - Lake City.**

*"Dr. Lee Brown's The Invitation beautifully expresses the heart of the Lord, inspiring me to fully embrace my identity in Him. I wholeheartedly recommend this transformative book to anyone looking for an awakening of who we are in Jesus."* - **Eduardo Arroyo, Messianic Rabbi, Apologist, YouTuber**

*"Dr. Lee Brown has provided a much-needed resource for the church and beyond. This well written and informative book provides a sound guide for Christian growth though effective application of scripture and extra-biblical resources. Moreover, Dr. Brown offers his own vulnerability bridging the gap between doctrine and living the Christian walk!"*
- **Dr. David Jones, LPC - Associate Professor of Counselor Education and Family Studies, Liberty University, EdD, MPH, LPC.**

*"Dr. Lee Brown speaks of the hope that we have in Christ. He uses his own experiences to describe how we can teach and influence the next generation to have that same hope."*
– **Dr. Cathy Spark, LPC-S, LMFT-S, RPT-S**

*"A most compelling quote, for me, from this inspiring, informative book is: " The greatest aim of the enemy is not to get you to sin; it's to cause you to forget who you are." Dr. Lee Brown was clearly inspired by God to challenge and encourage new and long-time Christians to go deeper in our understanding of who we really are in Christ. God confirmed and ignited important truths for me as I read The Invitation."*
- **Dr. Shannon Warden, Associate Professor of Counseling, Liberty University**

# Dedication

To my wife Kara who has sacrificed more than even I so that this book could be a written.

To my children, Avery and Emory, May God grant you hearts after Him secure in your heavenly identity and full of His love.

To my parents who raised me in the way I should go and never withdrew their support and care.

To my nana who showed me what it looks like to be selfless and generous in every way.

To Jesus, my King and my brother, may your name be honored and revered.

To my Father in Heaven may you be glorified, and your people edified by this book.

Scan the QR code for a free Study Guide!

or visit:

https://www.truepotentialmedia.com/invitation/

# Contents

| | |
|---|---|
| Preface | 9 |
| 1. What is an Identity? | 13 |
| 2. What We Were and What We Became | 23 |
| **Category One: An Inheritance** | **39** |
| 3. Becoming His Inheritance | 41 |
| 4. The Invitation | 53 |
| **Category Two: Citizens** | **65** |
| 5. The Kingdom | 67 |
| 6. The True Ecclesia | 81 |
| 7. Three Dimensions of Citizenship | 93 |
| **Category Three: Disciples** | **107** |
| 8. A Vision for Becoming | 109 |
| 9. Why A Disciple? | 125 |
| **Category Four: Children** | **137** |

| | |
|---|---|
| 10. Child: What is My Father Like? | 139 |
| 11. The Profound Revelation of Adoption | 155 |
| 12. Privileges, Obligations, and Inheritances | 165 |
| About the Author | 177 |

# Preface

The writing of this book spawned from a very unexpected nudge by a dear friend, Steve Spillman. I was working on finishing a dissertation and launching a non-profit among many other things and writing a book certainly wasn't on my list of ambitions. One day I received a call from Steve to casually talk about a variety of interests when toward the end of the call Steve asked, "Lee, if you were going to write a book this year what would it be about?" I'm not sure if it was out of insanity or simply the divine graces of God, but somehow in the midst of all that was weighing on my shoulders I gave Steve an answer knowing exactly where it would lead next. "Lee, you need to write that book!" he said. "Yea, I was afraid you'd say that, Steve, thanks." I lead the preface with this story because you need to know that this book wouldn't be in your hands without Steve's encouragement and generosity to pull out of me something that I might have kept to myself for far too long. I hope it blesses you.

## *The* INVITATION

The concept of one's identity in Christ is perhaps one of the most widely talked about concepts among churches, yet I'm convinced, it is still the least understood. How can I make such a claim? Simply because one mustn't look far to see that those who profess to be "in Christ" simply do not live like it. It is like a king who lives as a commoner in a land he was meant to rule. Furthermore, as another litmus test, I ask, "how would the world look if Christian's were in fact fully living and leading from a secure place in knowing their identity?" I'm not sure entirely the answer to that question, but something tells me it would look a lot different from the world we're living in right now.

I believe a key contributor to this dilemma stems from the reality that the vast majority of the church's teachings on one's identity in Christ is most often steeped in religious vernacular and symbolisms that leave many scratching their heads. Additionally, many of our teachings are found lacking practicality in how one's identity ought to effect everyday life. In this book it is my aim to simply crack the surface and lay the foundational groundwork for better understanding and thus living out one's identity in Christ. I do not think that this work will be "better" than any work that has come before me nor any work to come after, I just believe it may be helpful for others who share my style of learning and comprehension.

Before beginning you should know that I do not intend to cover every nuance, aspect, or angle that one could possibly conjure up regarding one's identity. In fact, I have intentionally chosen to leave out many of the most talked about aspects of our identity simply to avoid offering information that has been offered many times before.

## Preface

Instead, this project seeks to pull out new insights and meaning from Scripture's teachings that have not previously been emphasized, at least so far as I am aware. Furthermore, I have tried my best to wage war on ambiguity and offer forth practical ways in which our identity ought to effect daily living. My prayer is that from a proper insight into who one is, a new way of living might emerge. A way of living that is full of power, peace, joy, and righteousness.

Throughout the book you will notice a multitude of quotes. That is because one, I simply love quotes; I find they have a beautiful and poetic way of communicating things that would otherwise be quite bland. Secondly, it is because each author has contributed in some way, great or small, to my own personal journey and I am indebted to their spiritual pioneering before me. Two of the most influential voices that you will hear me quote are Dan Mohler and Dallas Willard. Both have been influential to me beyond articulation so much so that I'm not sure who I would be today without their influence in my life.

I pray you enjoy and accept "The Invitation"

# 1. What is an Identity?

*"Unlike a drop of water which loses its identity when it joins the ocean, man does not lose his being in the society in which he lives. Man's life is independent. He is born not for the development of the society alone, but for the development of his self."* - B. R. Ambedkar

Over the last several years, there has been an uptick in conversation surrounding our identity in Christ. It has become a somewhat trendy topic among Christians, and for good reason! The concepts of identity are foundational, and without them, it will be impossible to live the abundant life Christ made provisions for through His death, resurrection, and ascension to the throne. Yet, as important as the topic is and as trendy as it has become, we are still lacking quality resources giving attention to our identity. I'd argue that much (certainly not all) of what has been written up to this point on the topic comes up short. While the content is packed with truth, much of it remains vague or littered with spiritualized jargon that has rendered the powerful concepts within useless, almost like a treasure chest that has only been halfway unearthed. The truth remains stuck in the pages rather than being lived out by the readers.

Is that a bold claim? Perhaps, but I believe it's true. For instance, an estimated 31.6% of the global population identifies as Christian, yet the evidence of such a Christian population is lacking.[1] By this, we can see that many of today's Christians have not been taught *who they are* as a result of Christ's work. I once heard it said, "A pound of meat would surely be affected by a quarter pound of salt." If nearly a third of the earth's population is "Christian"—and by that, I mean those who intend to follow Jesus into His way of living through utter reliance upon and allegiance to Him as Lord and Savior—then where is the overwhelming impact of those identified as the "salt of the earth"?

**The Real Issue**

> I believe that what we have is an identity problem.

Now, I'm not a betting man, but I sure would bet that our problem is not a theology problem (though there's plenty of that going around). Further, I don't think we are lacking in evangelism, church planting, or missional outreach initiatives. I believe that what we have is an identity problem. We have self-proclaimed Christians who lack clarity on what it means to be *in Christ* and for Christ to be *in them.* Worse yet, many lack the understanding

[1] Statista. "Share of Global Population by Religion 2022." ( 2024.) https://www.statista.com/statistics/374704/share-of-global-population-by-religion/

## What is an Identity?

of who Christ has invited them to become through the cross, resurrection, and the transformative power of His Spirit. The enemy has many of our minds caught up on what God must want us to *do* rather than on who God wants us to *become*.

The teaching of the early church fathers was clear: The disciples of Jesus (that's you and me) who lived after He ascended to heaven were to act as a continuation of His incarnation on the earth. Here's the important part: becoming like Jesus and living according to the culture of His kingdom doesn't just happen by accident. Just like a young quarterback who aspires to be like Tom Brady cannot reach their goal simply by "believing" he's like Tom Brady, neither can a Christian expect to mature into Christlikeness, nor walk in Christ's power and victory in this life, without a plan and intentional effort. Yes, that plan must include proper theology. But without grasping the foundational teaching of one's identity—who we are, who we are not, and who we are becoming—we will never experience the Kingdom life of *power* that Christ provides for us today.

**What is True Power?**

Before I continue, I'd like to clear up what I mean by "power." Depending on your background, you may associate the term power with signs, wonders, and energetic worship gatherings. Though these things are displays of power, they are not where I wish to draw your attention. Instead, by the phrase "Kingdom life of power," I simply mean life in line with the character and nature of Jesus. It's about being the type of person who has peace when anxiety should otherwise be overwhelming. Now that's power! As a counselor, I often ask clients this question: "Which is the better goal, to live a life with no storms or to become the type of person who can sleep in the midst of them?"

The Kingdom life can take other forms too. It may also look like kindness when cruelty should be present, or gentleness instead of vengeance. Kingdom power is the ability to give out of your lack in order to sustain and comfort your enemy. But then it is also the ability to exercise self-control while being disciplined in humility.

Living in this kind of power doesn't just happen overnight. We cannot simply "accept" Christ at church on Sunday and then wake up on Monday completely transformed. The process is long, hard-fought, and requires a great deal of intentionality, endurance, and effort. However, the impending danger is this: if we do not recognize the truth about our identity, we will more than likely end our Christian walk right where it began, having never advanced into true freedom. When I speak of a powerless Christian, I do not mean one who is lacking in signs and wonders; I mean someone in whom Christ is no longer being continually formed (Galatians 4:19). Someone who no longer has the impactful effect of salt on meat or light in darkness. Someone whose faith no longer works through love (Galatians 5:6), and someone who lives more from their human nature than their holy nature.

Finally, the power we experience is His energy working within us and through us. The apostle Paul says it this way: *"To this end I also labor, striving with all <u>His energy working powerfully within me</u>."* (Colossians 1:29) Any fruit that is to come from our lives is His power married

## What is an Identity?

together with our faith and effort. While someone may hold onto their faith in Christ without grasping their identity, no one can successfully apply effort without knowing their identity. If an athlete didn't know what kind of athlete they were, they would not know how they ought to train to succeed as an athlete. Are they a runner or a cyclist? In this case, someone may identify and have faith that they are an athlete until the day they die, but it does not make them an accomplished or effective athlete of any kind.

> **If a Christian is unclear on their identity, they will be unclear on how to live.**

In the same way, identifying as a Christian is equivalent to identifying as an athlete. It's a broad term that needs to be clarified. If a Christian is unclear on their identity, they will be unclear on how to live. Kings don't live like peasants unless, of course, they simply don't know that they are a king. If a Christian is unclear on how to live, they may still enter eternal life, but they will die as one through whom Christ was never formed and thus fruit was never produced. The Bible is clear that a fruitless life will have eternal effects. Without knowing how to live, a Christian will live as a powerless Christian, having never experienced the abundant life made available to them. We must remember that we are to be co-laborers with Christ as rulers, stewards, and mature light bearers who produce with authority fruit that glorifies the Father. The vision the enemy has for your life is one that strips you of these things.

## *The* INVITATION

There is hope, however, and that is precisely what this book aims to offer: hope and empowerment that leads to an effective life in Christ. You can live an abundant life in this broken and chaotic world, but only through following Christ into the Kingdom life He made available. This will require seeing yourself for who you truly are and who you are not. It will require you to know your purpose. Finally, as a by-product of understanding your identity, you will begin to understand God's will for your life and what it is He'd like you to do. However, I must caution you that any attempts to discover what God would like you to *do* outside of who God would like you to *become* will be met with frustration and, eventually, in some cases, depression.

I will try my best throughout the coming pages to present as clearly as I can what I believe the Bible teaches about our identity in Christ. It is my special aim to wage war against ambiguity and to create a deep sense of clarity through defining terms such as the one we've used numerous times already: "identity in Christ." What does it mean, and what are its implications in everyday living? Furthermore, practicality is another special aim I have, because what good is knowledge that cannot be expressed and put into practice?

There are four attributes we will explore together as it relates to who you are in Christ. Each has extremely important implications that will affect the quality of your life in Christ, and thus they should not be cherry-picked but rather seen as four interlocking strands that support each other and require each other for success. The four areas of identity we will explore together do not make up the totality of our identity. Instead, this book will serve

## What is an Identity?

as a foundational building block. It should be viewed as content that can (and should) be built upon, but at the same time, should you never read another book on spiritual identity, you will still have what you need to live a power-filled and productive life in Christ as He is formed within you.

**Defining an Identity**

To wrap up our introductory chapter, I must share what I mean when I use the term "identity." Since it is the central topic, we must lay the groundwork here for what is to come. If you take the time to run a simple Google search on the definition of "identity," you will quickly notice, as with all words, there is no single official definition; rather, we are met with a host of sources all trying to say in the best way they can what is meant by the word "identity." It is the work of philosophers to take something immaterial, such as one's identity, and give it substance through words. I will attempt to do no different here. To begin, since I am a counselor and mostly work in the fields of psychology and Biblical studies, I will begin by sharing The American Psychological Association's (APA) definition, and then I will share a more precise definition of identity as it relates to this book and a spiritual level.

The APA gives the following definition of identity:

> "An individual's sense of self is defined by (a) a set of physical, psychological, and interpersonal characteristics that is not wholly shared with any other person and (b) a range of affiliations (e.g., ethnicity) and social roles. Identity involves a sense of continuity or the feeling that one is the same person today that one was

yesterday or last year (despite physical or other changes). Such a sense is derived from one's body sensations; one's body image; and the feeling that one's memories, goals, values, expectations, and beliefs belong to the self. Also called personal identity."[2]

I share this first so that we might first see how the 21st-century secular world defines one's identity and how it compares or contrasts with what the true essence of an identity is according to God's design. The first error we must address is that the APA reduces identity down to one's sense of self based on things that can change or are simply not that important (physical, psychological, and interpersonal characteristics). There are two issues here: first, identity is not concluded based on senses, and second, your identity is not *defined* by physical, psychological, or interpersonal characteristics. If identity is a matter of the senses, then one is likely to have a new identity at different stages throughout life. That, my friends, is what we call an identity crisis, and it is paralyzing, not empowering.

> Identity is a matter of reality, not a matter of the senses.

Would you believe that the vast majority of clients who come to visit have come because they lack the understanding of who they are, and they most often have no idea that's their primary issue? No, identity is a matter of reality, not a matter of the senses. Let me use an illustration: if a king made a poor choice that led to the death of many

---

2   "APA Dictionary of Psychology." (2024) https://dictionary.apa.org/.

citizens, he may sense in a moment of great despair that he was never meant to be king and that perhaps he was wired with a personality that is better suited for a servant who follows orders rather than a leader who makes decisions. No matter if his "sense of self" identifies as a king or a servant, reality says he is a king and he must show up to fulfill a king's duties because no one else can. This is the essence of how identity works. The material characteristics mentioned above (physical, psychological, and interpersonal) are *defined by our identity*, not the other way around.

We must then ask, "Where do we inherit our identity?" Much like morals, our identity must be assigned by a higher authority, that is, a creator. The same person who defines right from wrong must also define the identity of His creation. The core issue at hand is "Who is going to be your God?" "On whose authority are you going to rely?" If you were created, then only the creator can decide your identity, but if you are only a "cosmic accident," then you can be your own god and decide for yourself things such as right vs. wrong and even your own identity.

Let's briefly discuss the definition of identity that I wish to work with for the remainder of this book. You should know I do not consider myself a philosopher, but I am going to attempt to do a philosopher's work here due to its importance.

> *The identity is the essence of a person that defines their authority, behavior/character, purpose, and rights. It is the reality from which a person is informed on their place, and function in a family or society.*

With this working definition in mind, it is easy to see how one who is lacking in their understanding of identity is more likely to live a life of powerlessness, fruitlessness, and suffering in their mind, emotions, and body. As I noted earlier, our creator must define these things for us, and we must accept them and learn to walk in them since who (not what) we are called, created, and designed to be is contrary to our fallen nature which wages war on God's redemptive process. This means we may not *feel* the same way God sees us, yet reality remains despite our feelings. We are indeed who He says we are, but whether we choose to walk in it is up to us. The old adage rings true, "you can lead a horse to water, but you can't make it drink." Join me now as we dive deep into God's plan for us as children, citizens, disciples, and inheritance.

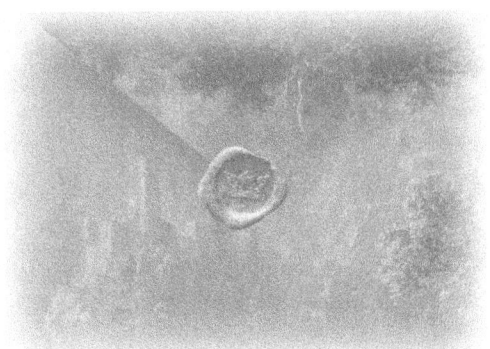

# 2. What We Were and What We Became

*"The fall of man is written in too legible characters not to be understood: Those that deny it, by their denying, prove it."* - George Whitefield

Before we begin our discussion on who we are in Christ, we must spend time exploring who we are outside of Christ and how we inherited such a status. Further, we must spend time understanding God's original intention, that is, His desire for us at the time of creation as it relates to our identity. This will help us to see more clearly that by default, mankind is no longer what God intended us to be, and it will give us a blueprint for who we are becoming in Christ since the story of the gospel is one of restoration and renovation.

Now, to clarify more terms. When I say *"in Christ,"* I mean to say *in a covenant relationship with Christ*. And by that I am referring to one has placed complete reliance upon and allegiance to Jesus as king, savior, and Lord and continues to live in such a way. Likewise, when I speak of being *"outside of Christ,"* I am speaking of those *outside of a covenant relationship.* To some, this may seem obvious; however, to many, the phrase "identity in Christ" requires clarity, and since everything we will speak on henceforth is contingent upon being in Christ, I believe it is important to bring clarity to this issue. Therefore, when we speak of our identity in Christ, we are speaking about our authority, behavior/character, purpose, and rights, as well as our place and function in family or society as determined by our creator for those who are in covenant relationship with Christ. In the same manner, when we speak of our identity outside of Christ, we are referring to the same thing but for those not in a covenant relationship with Christ.

We will quickly see that there are extreme implications for the present life, not merely the age to come, that are drastically different depending on whether one is in Christ or outside of Christ. Those outside of Christ do not have the same identity as those in Christ; therefore, they do not have the same authority, behavior/character, purpose, or rights, nor do they have the same place and function in family or society. Hopefully, you are beginning to see that the same "identity in Christ" that has for so many Christians remained vague and largely spiritual, in fact, has profound practical implications for everyday living.

**God's Original Intent**

We must understand God's original intention because in seeing it, we will also see that we are a galaxy away from it in the worst kind of way. This revelation of what we were meant to be and what we have become is the first step in grasping the power and love within redemption. To discover God's original intention for His human creation, we must go back to the beginning. Identity and purpose are interlocked. If you wish to discover your purpose, look to understand your identity. The opposite is also true: if you can identify why you exist, then you will be well on your way to discovering all the other elements involved with your identity. Lucky for us, the Word of God shares with us in explicit detail both who we are and our many purposes for existing. As you'll see, or perhaps have already come to realize, our identity is not a one-stop shop. There are many layers to who we are and with that many purposes, roles, responsibilities, and commands we must fulfill. Do not fear, however, because with our identity comes not just the responsibilities to fulfill, but also the authority and the energy to fulfill them.

Let's begin by asking then, what is it that God intended for humans to do? Is the human existence best summed up as the duration of time in which a person must endure the process of eating, sleeping, working, paying bills, overcoming ailments, suffering crises, making memories, and hoping all this happens with as little misery as possible? There must be more meaning to our existence. Indeed, for the one who adopts God's Word as true, there is much more meaning to our time on the earth. "In the beginning, God created..." and like every creator, He created with a purpose in mind. Even if an artist claims that there was no real purpose for their latest creation, all that tells us is that they have not come to a firm conclusion as to their purpose for creating, but there was indeed a purpose, or they would have not gone through the effort to bring into existence what was previously only in their mind. In the same way, God created man; therefore, we must seek His purpose in doing so, for though we do not know immediately why, we do know that there is a reason. Take a moment to be encouraged. If you are here reading this book, you too have been created by a creator, which means your very existence has a purpose. Just because you are still seeking it out doesn't mean it's not there.

So then, why did God create humankind?

> *Then God said, "Let us make man in our image, after our likeness, to rule over the fish of the sea and the birds of the air, over the livestock, and over all the earth itself and every creature that crawls upon it... God blessed them and said to them, 'Be fruitful and multiply, and fill the earth and subdue it; rule over the fish of the sea and the birds of the air and every creature that crawls upon the earth.'"* (Genesis 1:26, 28)

The first purpose for humankind we must address is God's intent for humans to rule, multiply, and reign. Though we will unpack this in much greater depth when we discuss citizenship and the Ecclesia, I must spend a short time addressing it here. Some may say we're still subduing the earth; after all, we are at the top of the food chain, and we continue to advance civilization via animal domestication and technological advancements. However, what matters is not that these things are being done but rather how they are being done and in what spirit. One need not look far to see that many, if not most of these things are being done in the spirit of greed, not generosity, and for selfish gain rather than love. For example, much of our infrastructure before machinery and even today much of our food is established on the backs of animals treated without dignity. Additionally, in much of the world today, our most advanced technology, furniture, and even everyday effects are established at the expense of those subject to forced labor camps. In many cases, we are exploiting the vulnerable and needy so that the wealthy might have more. This specific offense was often highlighted in God's rebukes of His people in ancient Israel (See especially Proverbs 14:31; 22:16, 22-23, Ezekiel 16:49; 22:29). I can't imagine it has become any less repulsive to Him today. So yes, we are still, in many respects, subduing the earth, but entirely in the wrong way.

Though God is likely sorrowful beyond description at how humanity rules, He is not angry, at least with those who rule this way and are outside of a covenant relationship with Christ. He knows that fallen humans will live and act like fallen humans. It is with those who ought to know better and who ought to live differently as a result of their new identity that He finds Himself angry, that is, should they continue to live according to their old nature. A brilliant illustration of this is that of the Pharisees. As far as I can see, the only people Christ grew angry with while on the earth were these "spiritually elite" teachers of the law. These were the ones who should have been teaching the people of Israel who they were in relation to

YHWH their God and how they were to live as a result. Yet, they were blinded by their pride and in turn led the people of Israel straight into spiritual bondage through their legalistic teachings that focused more on *doing* than *becoming*.

> The entire story from beginning to end is about the kingdom and its establishment upon the earth.

The idea that Jesus was the first to bring the kingdom to earth and make it available is derived from a failure to see that, from the first page of the Bible to its last, the central theme is centered around establishing a physical kingdom in the material world that looks and operates just like God's kingdom that was preexistent in the immaterial world. The entire story from beginning to end is about the kingdom and its establishment upon the earth. It was birthed in the Garden, and like anything that is birthed, it begins in the infancy stage. When we are instructed not to despise small beginnings (Zechariah 4:10), we can look back and see that even God, instead of establishing a massive kingdom for Himself on the earth (which He could have easily done), chose to begin small and set up His kingdom in a Garden. Before the Garden could expand, a divine adversary thwarted God's plan for advancement, at least temporarily. How did this villain accomplish such a feat? Through stripping God's rulers of their proximity to Him, thus eliminating their source of energy and authority to expand the kingdom. In effect, he disconnected the light bulb from the socket in which it must remain in order to give off its light. Though Adam and Eve did not die in a physical sense, much like an unscrewed light bulb doesn't cease to be a light bulb, they did perish in another sense.

## Ye Shall Surely Die

Prior to the fall, Adam and Eve lived with what I refer to as a whole soul. For simplicity's sake, the soul refers to the total human being and all its parts. It is the faculty of the human that integrates all the other human faculties (i.e., body, mind, and spirit). In order to have a whole soul or an *abundant life* as Jesus calls it, one must be whole in all their faculties. There are more than three, but for our purposes, those faculties consist of the body, mind, and spirit. God is spirit (John 4:24), and therefore our interaction with Him and His kingdom is first and foremost on a spiritual level. If our spirit is disconnected from His Spirit and His spiritual kingdom, then we are in essence dead, and the rest of our human faculties will begin to follow suit. Our thoughts, beliefs, worldviews, emotions, behaviors, habits, and character will manifest in the material world what is true of the condition of our spirit in the immaterial world.

If we take away branches from a plant, it may go on living with little adverse effect compared to the taking away of an arm or a leg from a human. That is because the loss of a branch is not as impactful on the overall quality of life as the loss of bodily members, namely because an arm is more helpful to the human than a branch is to a plant. The more helpful an object is for one's quality of life, the greater the loss, and eventually with enough loss, something is deemed *ruined or lost*. Think of what we label a car that has been totaled; we refer to it as a "total loss."

When Adam and Eve "died," they were in essence corrupted and totally lost because the most essential and helpful faculty of their person, the spirit, was disconnected from its most vital source of nutrients, God and His Kingdom. Because the spirit of a person is interconnected to the other faculties, when it is corrupted, the other members will be as well. The social dimension, the physical dimension, and the psychological dimension of the self are all affected by the spiritual dimension. Anything that exudes from our lives that is unlike God or His kingdom originates from a spirit that is experiencing spiritual deprivation. Our spirit must be regenerated, born again as it were, in order to progress towards the abundant life (in every dimension named above) that Jesus made provisions for. Therefore, when the Bible says we are born into iniquity (Psalm 51:5), it is describing the status or the condition in which we enter the earth. We, by default, are born with a corrupt, totally lost spirit that is in essence missing the mark so far as it relates to God's intentional design and purpose for us. Therefore, we are born into a state of being that is inclined to sin since the spirit is, from conception like Adam, disconnected from an Edenic relationship with God and His kingdom.

## Children of Light and the Imago Dei

At this point, we have explored God's intent for humans as rulers in God's kingdom on earth. We have also explored briefly how God's intentions were thwarted in Eden and where the fall of Adam leaves us in terms of our status and identity upon conception. Though it is wonderful that God intends for humans to rule as kings, this aspect of our original identity isn't the singular nor most valuable component of God's original intent for us;

there is much more. In addition to rulers, God also desired children because, as we'll see in greater depth later, the role of children is crucial in expanding a kingdom. I'd like to share with you a few key points about the significance of children that you should hold onto for our deep dive in the coming chapters.

First, a child was to be, in essence, a clone of their father. They were expected to think like and behave like their father, no matter if that was their biological father or their spiritual father. This is why Jesus said *"...if Abraham were your father, you would be doing the works Abraham did."* (John 8:39) And again, Paul says, *"Follow God's example as dearly beloved children."* (Ephesians 5:1) It is precisely at this junction we discover the significance of not only our relationship to God as children but also why He found it appropriate to take the dust of the earth and fashion it into something that would bear His image. His image, of course, is most often summed up in one word: light. He is the Father of lights, and He is light (1 John 1:5-7; James 1:17-18). *Light* is a word used through scripture that refers primarily to a knowledge of the truth and faith working through love (Galatians 5:6). Jesus tells us to let our *"...light so shine before men that others may see your good works and glorify your Father in Heaven."* (Matthew 5:16) The 'light' Jesus is referring to is your faith in the knowledge of the truth working through you to display the character and nature of your Father to the world around you. God's character and nature is anything consistent with righteousness and

> His image, of course, is most often summed up in one word: light.

love, and as His children, we will learn to think like Him and behave like Him.

## Children, a Means for Expansion

As rulers and image bearers, God intended for us to be co-laborers with Him on the earth. Through their intimate relationship and close proximity to God in the Garden, Adam and Eve were to be like their Father as they learned His nature via intimate interaction with Him, and then they were to "fill the earth" with it. The idea was that God would expand His kingdom, which was initially only present in the Garden, throughout the rest of the world over time. What was God's strategy for His initiative of global expansion? His strategy was childbearing.

> *Has not the LORD made them one, having a portion of the Spirit? And why one? Because He seeks godly offspring. So guard yourselves in your spirit and do not break faith with the wife of your youth.* (Malachi 2:15)

Children were the primary means for expanding a king's domain. Consider, for example, how Jacob, who was later renamed Israel, became a nation. It was through his sons who became the patriarchs of the nation's twelve tribes. Kingdoms were, in essence, families that grew and expanded until they took dominion over more and more land. When a land was conquered, the culture of that family—its laws, customs, values, and celebrations—became the new reality. This is what God had in mind when He commanded Adam and Eve to *"…be fruitful and multiply… fill the earth and subdue it."*

**The Origins of Discipleship**

There is, however, one critical detail we mustn't overlook. Some may say it's a problem or, at a minimum, an extreme inconvenience for successful and efficient kingdom expansion, but God isn't threatened by it; in fact, He intentionally designed it. That is the mere fact that when children, who are the primary means of expansion, are born, they are born immature. It takes a child quite some time to mature, and what's more problematic is maturity isn't guaranteed nor is it automatic, and it certainly isn't a quick process. A child's maturity requires learning and training, which requires a teacher and a trainer. As humans, we must undergo a maturing and a formation process in every faculty of the self; that is to say, we must mature and undergo a formation in our bodies, mindset, social intellect, and spirit. Formation is inevitable and we each will be formed; the question is by whom or what will we be formed? Hitler underwent spiritual formation and a maturing process, as did Billy Graham and Gandhi. Each was formed and shaped into the person they became, which was characterized by their morals, ethics, behaviors, intentions, and desires. How is it one man can desire the mutilation of an entire race while another loves even those who torture and kill their loved ones? The answer is formation.

This process of shaping begins in the womb and carries on throughout life. Although it is true that as we age the formation of our spirit cements into place like handcrafted pottery, it is always possible for someone to be reformed no matter what age; at some point, however, it may require a willingness to break and, in some cases, be completely shattered. This is often why God will find people in their lowest and darkest moments because they now have a soft, pliable heart that can be worked with and reformed. If one keeps a soft heart through a posture of humility, they will find the ongoing formation and maturing process that continues throughout life is much easier to navigate.

> God designed the expansion of His kingdom to work through childbearing and childcaring.

God designed the expansion of His kingdom to work through childbearing and childcaring.

*I have chosen him so that he will <u>command his children and his household</u> after him to <u>keep the way of the LORD by doing what is right and just</u>, so that the LORD may bring upon Abraham what He has promised."* (Genesis 18:19)

He could have simply established a process in which the earth would be automatically populated by mature and spiritually formed humans without the process of growing pains, yet He elected otherwise. Why do you suppose that is? It would most certainly be much faster to expand the kingdom, and it would have come with way fewer errors since we know that the maturing process is full of mistakes. The reason for God's choice here is likely multifaceted and well beyond my ability to comprehend; however, I have a few observations that may clue us in.

First, in the years in which we must raise a child, we also learn, or at least we are supposed to learn, to walk in a high level of selflessness that can only be learned in the process of caring for a child. If you have raised children, you no doubt know what I mean. Second, we learn best by teaching others. In high school, I played four years of varsity football. As a soccer player, I naturally fit in at the kicking position, and through years of hard work and training, I became efficient. Around my junior year, my kicking coach implemented a new training exercise that admittedly had me scratching my head, that is until I saw the results of regularly engaging in the exercise. My coach told me that I had reached a point in my maturity as a kicker and that I must now begin to teach a younger prospect the fundamentals. I learned quickly that through teaching what I had been taught, I was able to improve my performance as a kicker. Somehow through teaching, I was reinforcing in myself principles that enabled me to perform at a higher level.

Similarly, when we teach the next generation the ways of our God and His kingdom, we not only contribute to their formation in a manner that aligns with Heaven, but we also reinforce in ourselves principles of who we are and how we ought to live, resulting in more maturity. Through the process of child-raising, we see that God designed in the fabric of the universe the act of disciple-making, though, of course, this term didn't come around until much later in history. Nevertheless, as we discovered in Genesis 18:19 above, discipleship begins in our homes, and that is precisely how God intended it. The advancement of the kingdom on earth relies on it. It is a widely accepted idea in science and scholarship that the adult we end up becoming is heavily affected by the environment and experiences of our childhood. My father always referred to young children as wet cement, and he is right. It is during these years when children are impressionable that we must lay foundations that will shape the rest of their lives. It is for us as parents to choose the direction in which their formation goes. We are to govern strictly the influences our children are exposed to. Those influences may include teachers, peers, shows, games, and people we allow them around unattended; the list is endless.

**Our Default Identity of Corruption**

Up to this point, we have examined in brief a few core aspects of our identity as God intended from the onset of creation. We were created to be mature light-producing children of God who rule and reign with God over the earth in His likeness, all the while expanding territory through discipling our children into mature image bearers who likewise go and do the same. However, due to the fall, we are born corrupt and ruined. In other words, the identity we were supposed to have, we are not born with. What then are we born into?

First, instead of rulers, we are born into slavery. We are slaves to the flesh and its harmful passions, causing us to sin and suffer death. We are slaves to the pain of childbearing and the taxing labor now required for survival. We are slaves in our minds and emotions to tormenting thoughts and feelings. We are not free, but there is a truth that sets captives free.

Second, instead of being children of God, we are children of Satan, in that we are inclined to do the will of Satan before the will of God. It is just as Jesus told the Pharisees, *"You are of your father the devil, and your will is to do your father's desires."* (John 8:44) Some might consider this to be the status of an orphan since as a child of the devil one is without care, direction, support, or love, which are essential pillars a father provides.

Third, instead of walking in the light as image bearers, we reside in the dark. The apostle Paul writes to Ephesus saying,

> *For at one time you were darkness, but now you are light in the Lord. Walk as children of light (for the fruit of light is found in all that is good and right and true)."* (Ephesians 5:8-9: see also 1 John 1:5-7, 1 Thessalonians 5:5)

We are blind, unable to discern the truth, thus rendering us a total loss in need of redemption. Jesus' redemptive work on the cross made provisions for an abundant life in the midst of a broken world. It secured our ability to be restored to the identity God intended for us in this life and in the age to come. In this life we can progress towards complete restoration through the Spirit's work of sanctification, but there is a day coming of complete transformation, and once we are fully restored and renovated, He will receive for Himself His inheritance, which is the saints. Our full renovation, though it will be complete at His second coming, begins today, and we can resume our place as citizens, children, disciples, and His inheritance on this earth, and when we do, we will bear His light, thus successfully expanding His kingdom on the earth as in Heaven.

# Category One: An Inheritance

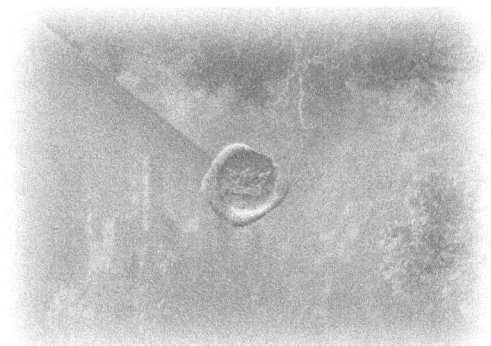

# 3. Becoming His Inheritance

*Every human being is in a state of becoming, of passing from what he was to what he is to be... Not only are we all in the process of becoming; we are becoming what we love* – A.W. Tozer

*"To become what we are capable of becoming is the only end in life."* – Robert Louis Stevenson

### A Piece of My Story

When I was twenty-four, I received an opportunity to take a dream job. Well, at least it was a dream job according to my naive and immature understanding. At the time, I wanted to climb the ladder of the church world. I wanted to preach all over the world and eventually lead a large church. I wanted to rub shoulders with all the Christian big-name leaders and influencers with the hopes of "building the Kingdom." It didn't help that I had a background in theater and thus I could put on a show when speaking. On stage, I could captivate a room, but off stage, I had the emotional intelligence and all-around maturity of... well... a child. The wild part is, just like 99.9% of young aspiring Christian leaders today and even older ones, I had in my heart a genuine love for the Lord and a deep desire to glorify His name. The problem was, however, I had Lee in there as well. I had dreams and vision, something we've developed brilliant rhetoric for in the church world. We've celebrated it, and we even encourage these things as a mark of a good leader. There's a thin line we straddle here because God does indeed give vision to His children. He does fill their heart with dreams, but those visions don't produce within the child a self-sabotaging attitude of pride, greed, self-glorification, and success all in the name of His Kingdom.

> The litmus test to measure one's attitude in the midst of carrying a vision is to examine whether or not the vision carrier can lay down the vision with ease.

The litmus test to measure one's attitude in the midst of carrying a vision is to examine whether or not the vision carrier can lay down the vision with ease. Abraham was given a vision and a promise. That vision was one of natural impossibility considering it involved him and his wife having a son at the ripe age of 100. Indeed, he bore a son, and for years Abraham's heart must have blossomed with a vision for his future family. However, to ensure Abraham was not more interested in building His kingdom and cloaking it in "for your name's sake" jargon, God asked Abraham to surrender the vision by laying his son on the altar. Abraham reasoned within himself, "If my vision and dreams are to die... If my beloved son is to die... God is capable and indeed willing to raise them back to life again..." Was it easy? That's highly doubtful, but nevertheless, Abraham would pass the test.

It's a frightening idea to attend a church in which your spiritual leader would not be willing to lay down their 'church' and walk away. That means the leader is compromised, and instead of following them as they follow God, you're just following them right into the dreams of their heart. Yet, our nation is full of this scenario, and at twenty-four years old, I was well on my way to repeating the cycle. But God....

My wife and I, three months before having our first child, would move across the country to a place where we had no friends or family, to take a job at a church of 10,000. I would inherit a youth group larger than my previous church, and I was beyond excited, to say the least. We had hopes and dreams of making new memories and finding new friendships, but most importantly, we had high expectations for gaining Godly mentorship that would help us to cultivate our spiritual health, marital health, and leadership skills. Two months into the new role, reality hit. This place was not what I was told or sold in the recruiting process. The true colors were on full display, and I quickly began to realize I had made a mistake, or at a minimum, a gigantic miscalculation in my evaluation. Three months after our arrival, my campus pastor and his wife, who were big factors in our decision to take the position, would resign to assume leadership of another church. The resignation, however, was to my wife and me a resounding confirmation that our time would be coming to an end. Soon after, I had all the necessary conversations and established a 3-month off-boarding plan.

Defeated, confused, frustrated, broken, and resentful are a few of the words to describe my new emotional state. In the blink of an eye, my wife and I went from a hope-filled future to the inauguration of what would become one of the darkest and hardest seasons of our lives. During the 3-month off-ramp, the church provided me a gradual increase of "extra space" since they wanted to slowly remove my face from around campus. During that time, I would reconnect with the Lord since over the last year or so my prayer life had all but ceased (unless it was asking God to do something for us or the ministry) and my Bible study had become more about looking for content than about my own transformation. Over the next several months, the Lord would begin a transformational work in me that would hurt very badly for the next four to five years.

There are so many stories I wish I could share, but perhaps I will get that chance another time. For now, I'd just like to highlight how it all began, the spiritual transformation that is. On my twenty-fifth birthday at 4:30 am, the Lord would encounter me in an unreal way while I was holding my screaming two-month-old who had not slept all night. I was standing in our bathroom with the faucet running, rocking her as she wailed until finally, I heard a voice say, "Lee, You and Avery are not all that different. In the same way Avery is screaming uncontrollably, you also are just like her on the inside, and just like you are comforting her as she screams, so am I comforting you." At this, I most literally broke, and now I was debatably crying more profusely than my daughter. From this first of many breakings that would occur over the next several years, the Lord was able to deposit a message into my heart that I would either receive with humility or reject with pride, and depending on which I would choose, I believe would determine the course of my future.

As I mentioned before, I began to spend a lot of time in the Word during my off-boarding season. I wasn't allowed to preach anymore, so my reading was through a different set of eyes. I was reading for me this time and not for anyone else. I came across Jesus' warning to the church at Laodicea, and they hit me like a ton of bricks.

> *You say, "I am rich; I have grown wealthy and need nothing." But you do not realize that you are wretched, pitiful, poor, blind, and naked. I counsel you to buy from Me gold refined by fire so that you may become rich, white garments so that you may be clothed and your shameful nakedness not exposed, and salve to anoint your eyes so that you may see. Those I love I rebuke and discipline. Therefore, be earnest and repent.* (Revelation 3:17-19)

Jesus was speaking directly to me; I was the church of Laodicea. My place of employment wasn't the problem... The church was God's gracious gift and tool to get me where He needed me internally so that He could begin a transformational work. I was the religious leader who thought he was rich and well-clothed with all the insight in the world yet couldn't see his own nakedness and poverty. It was like someone turned the lights on and I could see myself as I truly was for the first time. It wasn't long after coming across this text that the Lord would highlight another:

> *Do not let your adorning be external—the braiding of hair and the putting on of gold jewelry, or*

*the clothing you wear— but let your adorning be the hidden person of the heart with the imperishable beauty of a gentle and quiet spirit, which in God's sight is very precious.* (1 Peter 3:3-4, ESV)

I realized then that in Revelation Jesus was speaking of the person of my heart, and boy was he in rough shape.

> He was calling me into the wilderness to be unknown to everyone but Him.

As Jesus commanded to the church of Laodicea, I repented. I chose then and there that I wanted to change. I wasn't sure what or how, but I knew God was speaking, and if nothing else, I was committed to listening. The next day I was administered the litmus test... Abraham (that's me in this case) was asked to crucify Isaac. God asked me to leave ministry as I had known it. He was calling me into the wilderness to be unknown to everyone but Him. The first practical display of obedience was to make a public post to my Instagram account—which as a twenty-four-year-old, was my source of affirmation and self-worth—that confessed the new revelations God had given me. I shared publicly that I had been like the recipient of Jesus' letter to the church of Laodicea and that I was now on a journey of repentance and surrender. I announced that I would be leaving ministry (my Isaac) and allowing God to do in me what He saw fit and well-pleasing. After this post went public, I was all but shunned (in a very nice and passive way, of course) by the community I once worshiped and served with. My follower count plummeted. Shallow, I know, but to me at that time, this was a big transition past the point of no return. I was committed to whatever God would have for me, and Isaac was officially on the altar. Little did I know that the hard stuff was still ahead of me, and to be honest, I'm glad I didn't know because I might not have given Him my 'yes'.

## The Revelation of Inheritance

The reason I shared a tiny piece of my story with you is to establish for you the context that will serve as the backdrop for the rest of this book. Walking in my identity as an inheritance is deeply personal to me, and by the end, I hope it will be for you too. It was in the midst of one of my lowest seasons that the revelation of my identity as His inheritance was given to me. I wish I could say it was a profound encounter with God on the top of a mountain in which He delighted in me and lavished me with compliments on how well I was doing and how proud He was of me for all I had given up. The reality is it wasn't that glamorous. It was a moment of rebuke rather than commendation.

I was experiencing a great deal of hardship; nothing was going right. Finances were worse than tight, marriage was on the rocks, stress was beyond articulation, and I wasn't sure how I could keep going. One evening I was in the shower praying, and by that, I mean, venting my stress. It had become a regular custom for me and yes, even though I was complaining, I felt God was a safe place for me and indeed He was and has been ever since. During my prayer, I asked God, "Lord please bless my life and please bless our endeavors." I was immediately convicted. The Lord gently spoke to my heart, "Lee, I have blessed you. Instead, you should be praying that your life would bless me and that your endeavors would bless me."

## *The* INVITATION

During that time, this sort of event was quite regular. God was actively changing the way I thought, and He was aggressively chiseling away at His inheritance. That'll make more sense in the next chapter.

Soon after this encounter with the Lord, He would lead me to Ephesians 1 in which Paul prays for you and me saying, *"I ask that the eyes of your heart may be enlightened, so that you may know the hope of His calling, the riches <u>of His glorious inheritance in the saints.</u>"* (Ephesians 1:18)

> To love is to will the good of another even at one's own expense.

"Lee, you are my inheritance. You were bought with a price. Yes, you have an inheritance too, but you only have an inheritance because you were first my inheritance." At this, a new prayer was birthed that I repeat often: "Father, I want to become everything your Son died for me to become." **If I am God's inheritance and I genuinely love Him, why wouldn't I want to become everything He died for me to become?** To love is to will the good of another even at one's own expense (more on this later). If I will the good of my Father, then I will naturally want Him to receive His inheritance in me and nothing less. It was from this moment on that I began to read the Bible with a completely different set of eyes. I no longer read the Bible as a manual of instructions for how to live, but rather I now saw it as a mirror of sorts. I saw it as a letter informing me on who I was. In the pages of scripture, I see who God is because Christ displayed Him without flaw or lack, for He is the visible image of the invisible God. If in Christ I see who God is and I am to be God's image bearer, then in Christ I also see who I am invited to become. Everything I was intended to be but am not because of Adam, I can now be once again in Christ, and it is precisely that which God seeks to inherit, that which was lost. In Christ, I most literally find myself. Now, I don't have to be offended at my neighbor because I'm not living for myself; I've died to myself and now I live for His name's sake. With each and every denial to my flesh, I am partaking in the sufferings that, like a chisel, will chip away at my fallen human nature until I become the wonderful masterpiece that resembles the Father.

A.W. Tozer's quote referenced in the chapter's opening becomes clear now: "...we are becoming what we love." Since I love the Father, I am driven with a deep unquenchable desire to become like Him and represent (that is to re-present) Him in the earth with my life. The more I look at Him, through His Word, Christ, and His creation, the more I love Him. The more I love Him, the more I desire to become like Him. The more I become like Him, the more I become love because He is love and as He is, so I am in the earth.

**Who Then Should I Be?**

Dr. Willard rightly said, "The main thing God gets out of your life is the person you become and that's the main thing you get out of it too." Who you become is both God's inheritance and your inheritance. This then begs a very important question: Who then ought we to become? Peter asks this question of his audience saying, *"Since everything will be destroyed in this way,"* referring to judgment day, *"What kind of people ought you to be?"* (2 Peter 3:11a). To avoid any confusion, Peter answers his question immediately:

## *The* INVITATION

> *You ought to conduct yourselves in holiness and godliness... Therefore, beloved, as you anticipate these things, make every effort to be found at peace—spotless and blameless in His sight.* (2 Peter 3:11b, 14)

This is God's original intention for his human image bearers: to be set apart from the way of the world (holy) and to be like Him (blameless). Paul reiterates this in his letter to the Ephesians, *"For He chose us in Him before the foundation of the world to be holy and blameless in His presence."* (Ephesians 1:4)

What kind of inheritance is Christ coming back for? What was it that He saw as He looked down the lanes of time that produced such a joy in Him that enabled Him to endure the cross? He saw a pure and spotless bride.

> *Husbands, love your wives, just as Christ loved the church and gave Himself up for her to sanctify her, cleansing her by the washing with water through the word, and to present her to Himself as a glorious church, without stain or wrinkle or any such blemish, but holy and blameless.* (Ephesians 5:25-27)

He died because when He looked deep into the future, He saw you, not living the life you've experienced up to this point with all of its agony and anguish. No, He saw you restored and established living in everything that the Father desired for you from before time began. That vision produced enough joy in the depths of His soul to enable Him to endure the cross. Despite this, He will not force it (i.e., salvation and sanctification) upon us. Instead, He freely invites us into it, risking rejection so that through our acceptance and willingness to endure the refining, He might experience love and joy simultaneously through our lives.

The question now becomes: are you a Christian for you or for Him? Is the promise of eternal life what you're after, or are you after being transformed into something eternal? Why are you in ministry or why do you desire to be in ministry? Don't you realize that your life is the primary ministry God calls you to and many neglect it in pursuit of something they think is more "significant"? The greatest mistake we make is believing the lie that anything in this life could be of more significance than who we become. In other words, we place more value on what we can do for God when He is more concerned with who we become as a consequence of remaining in Him. God is no prouder of Billy Graham than he is the pastor who faithfully stewarded a group of fifty people his entire life. God built both of those ministries, not their leaders, and a failure to recognize this causes many to associate the things they have done or been a part of in this life as a sign of competence, favor, or God's approval. Over the last few years, God has exposed many of the largest Christian leaders and their ministries from around the world. It has shown that the size of one's ministry or the amount of productivity they may have "for the kingdom" is not a result of someone's spiritual maturity. Woe to the one who cloaks the pursuit of their own dreams in the name of "for the kingdom". Your wildest dream should consist of becoming His inheritance, and anything that distracts you from that should be considered a threat that you're unwilling to put up with.

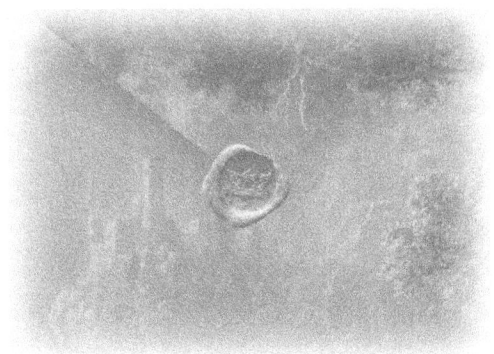

# 4. The Invitation

> *"No matter what man did from the Garden on, God never lost sight of what He made man to be... You're the pearl of great price to God the Father. That's not blasphemy. That's the gospel. You're the treasure in a field. To me He is, but to Him I am."*
> – Dan Mohler

As long as you base the value of your life on how things are going around you or the way you feel, the longer you will live enslaved to every passing thought and emotion. The hope of experiencing any degree of freedom or walking in any degree of authority in this world comes from the ability to base your value on the cross. But what does that even mean? Can we rid ourselves of the religious symbolisms? Yes! The cross was the price, and you were the prize. In the cross, we see a glimpse of the infinite value that we have in the eyes of the Father. As Dan Mohler asserts, "Why would He pay such a ridiculously high price as the blood of His Son to obtain you if He didn't think the purchased possession was worth it?"

> The Father does not base your worth on the person you are today; therefore, neither should you

The Father does not base your worth on the person you are today or the person you have been up to this point in your life; therefore, neither should you. The version of you that God finds irresistible is the version He saw from before time began. God predestined us to be His children, and as children, imitators of Him (image bearers) in all His glory. He is not surprised by the type of people we have become since the fall. The version of you that the enemy leverages to keep you bound in shame is the same version of you that God knew we'd all become due to the fall in Eden. The very thing you've been allowing to keep you from Him—that is, your feelings of being unworthy due to living like a type of person who acts "fallen"—is the very reason God desires you to draw near to Him.

There is a transformation process that must occur which will take us from the type of people we have been since birth into the type of people God desires to inherit. It is an ongoing process and will not be complete until the new age when the earth and all of creation are completely restored, but it begins now and God intends that we, once being born of the imperishable seed of His Spirit, will desire such a transformation. It is a baffling thing when someone finds deep shame in the type of person they are, yet they simultaneously do not desire to follow Christ into the new creation they could become. The invitation to follow Christ is not just an invitation into

Heaven, but more accurately to the biblical message, it is an invitation to get Heaven into you.

## How Does He Accomplish Our Transformation?

God's transformational work, theologically, is referred to as "sanctification", and while God has many ways of completing His good work in us, one method in particular takes before all the others. In the words of George Barlow, "The devil's way of extinguishing goodness is God's way of advancing it." The soil in which God grows a prosperous crop is often through the soil of persecution, trial, and refining. Personal hardships that appear devastating, if allowed, will lead us into spiritual growth, deeper faith, or greater compassion, advancing the transformation of our inner world.

When we study the lives of those who might be considered legends of our faith, people like Abraham, David, Daniel, Bonhoeffer, Corrie Ten Boom, the apostles, and others, we find a common thread. Each story is beautifully stained with trials, pain, and suffering. A great disservice to the modern-day body of believers, and quite frankly a result of chasing converts over disciples, is that we treat salvation like a sales pitch in which we highlight the best parts and leave out the core elements of what it means to follow Christ. The manner in which God transforms us is not exciting, and because there is little equipping, many fall away the moment it begins.

Now, to be clear, suffering is not unique to the Christian. Suffering is a part of this world and the delight of Satan. What is unique, however, is the result of suffering and our source of confidence while suffering. When one suffers, the only thing that matters is who or what their god is. If your god is money, it can't save you. If your god is your career, it will fail you. If drugs and alcohol are your god, they may numb the pain, but they'll kill you in the process. It's only when we look to God in our suffering that they can be taken and turned for good. We must embrace the suffering and trust the Lord will use it for our good, for as Peter says:

> *And after you have suffered for a little while, the God of all grace, who has called you to His eternal glory in Christ, will Himself restore you, secure you, strengthen you, and establish you.* (1 Peter 5:10)

## The Sculpture, the Gold, and the Clay

Scripture is abundant in its communication of how God transforms us into His glorious inheritance. We are likened to clay in the potter's hand, an ongoing work or masterpiece, and gold in a refiner's fire. These three metaphors paint for us pictures of our transformation process. First, each of us has a spirit that undergoes formation from the moment of conception. We are like wet pottery being molded by the world around us. Nurture, nature, and the forces of life have its formative effects. However, the hope of the believer is that God can in fact be the potter of our lives, that is, the type of person we become. When clay has been molded to the potter's satisfaction, it will undergo a process called "firing" in which it is heated to extreme temperatures for the purpose of cementing the vessel. However, in order for the clay to be cemented, something profound must occur in the clay. The purpose of the heat is singular. It exists to transform the clay into a completely new substance altogether. When the clay is subjected to fire, it undergoes a chemical change, in effect transforming the substance on a molecular level into an entirely new substance. It is no longer clay, for it has become ceramic. In the same way, the heat we encounter in life is utilized to transform us into new creations. It is, for this reason, that Paul proclaims, *"Therefore if anyone is in Christ, he is a new creation. The old has passed away. Behold, the new has come!"* (2 Corinthians 5:17) The new creation we're becoming is both our inheritance and God's.

Paul also likens us to a piece of art that an artist is continually working on so as to render it a masterpiece. He says, *"For we are God's workmanship, created in Christ Jesus to do good works, which God prepared in advance as our way of life."* (Ephesians 5:10) Now, I haven't a single cell in my body that possesses even the tiniest ability to create art, but I do love and appreciate it. My wife, however, is a wonderful artist, and her ability to create fascinates me and it provides me glimpses of the majesty of God our creator. When I consider works such as the Statue of David, Mt. Rushmore, and places like the Biltmore, I am left in a state of utter awe. I have often been moved by an artist's ability to create something out of nothing. The ability to transform a blank canvas into an image of wonder that has the power to evoke immense emotion is something I greatly appreciate. However, something that impresses me even more is when an artist can take a canvas that has been written off as ruined and turn it into a masterpiece. In more ways than you might realize, we can be likened to Michelangelo's statue of David in the artistic hands of God. Allow me to illustrate:

In the bustling city of Florence, where art whispered through cobblestone streets and the Arno carried dreams downstream, a massive block of Carrara marble lay abandoned. Weathered and battered by time, it bore the scars of disappointment. Two great sculptors had already attempted to wrest beauty from its core, only to leave it scarred and deemed irredeemable—a block ruined beyond salvation. It became a monument to failure, ignored by the very artisans who had once longed to shape it.

The marble, however, was not without ambition. Its icy veins still shimmered in the sunlight, whispering promises of greatness to any who dared to listen. For decades, it lay in quiet defiance, refusing to crumble under the weight of its rejection. The city's artists glanced past it, seeking marble less marred, less troublesome. It was simply too flawed, too fractured—until Michelangelo Buonarroti stood before it.

> Each blow liberated David from his marble prison, transforming imperfection into majesty.

At first, he did not see its faults. He saw only potential. In his mind's eye, he envisioned a figure trapped within, a biblical hero who would stand as a symbol of resilience and divine perfection. Michelangelo convinced the overseers of Florence to entrust him with the forsaken block, and in 1501, he began his work. For over two years, his chisel struck with relentless precision. Each blow liberated David from his marble prison, transforming imperfection into majesty. Michelangelo saw not the block's faults but the strength in its imperfections, shaping them into defiance: the furrowed brow, the poised sling, the towering stance.

## The Invitation

When unveiled in 1504, David was no mere statue—it was a testament to vision and perseverance, a triumph carved from a castaway stone. In Michelangelo's hands, the rejected marble became immortal, and the world saw not a flawed block but the glory it was always destined to become. In much the same way, we are like the beat-up, marred, and abandoned block of marble written off by society and perhaps even ourselves. But God, the author and perfecter of our faith, saw something in us that we didn't even see in ourselves and purchased us to begin His work in us. He didn't take a blank canvas but instead one deemed ruined and turned it into a masterpiece. Once complete, the image we become is both our inheritance and His.

Last, but certainly not least, we are likened to gold that undergoes the refiner's fire. The proverbial writer says it this way, *"A crucible for silver and a furnace for gold, but the LORD is the tester of hearts."* (Proverbs 17:3) To best illustrate the purpose of being likened to gold, allow me to share with you another story.

In the heart of a goldsmith's workshop, where the air shimmers with heat and the clang of hammers sings a song of transformation, raw gold begins its journey. Dug from the earth, it arrives veiled in impurities, its brilliance dulled by a host of imperfections. Yet within lies the promise of something radiant—a treasure waiting to emerge.

The goldsmith places the metal into the crucible, setting it atop the hungry flames. As the fire roars to life, the gold succumbs, melting into a molten pool. But this is not destruction; it is the beginning of rebirth. The heat

*The* INVITATION

intensifies, and the impurities rise to the surface—dark flecks that mar the golden glow. Patiently, the goldsmith skims them away, knowing that each pass of the ladle brings the gold closer to its truest self.

The process is relentless, the fire unwavering. The gold resists, its impurities clinging like shadows, but the goldsmith is unyielding. He knows the secret of refinement: only through the fire can the gold's purity be revealed. Time passes, the impurities diminish, and the molten gold begins to shine with an otherworldly clarity.

The goldsmith leans closer, his seasoned eyes searching the golden surface. He is not satisfied until he can see his own reflection, perfectly mirrored. This is the moment of truth, the sign that the gold has reached its utmost purity. No blemishes remain, only the brilliance of something made perfect through trial.

> In the fire's crucible, the gold has become a testament to the truth that beauty is forged through adversity...

The goldsmith smiles, for he has shaped not just metal but a symbol of endurance and transformation. In the fire's crucible, the gold has become a testament to the truth that beauty is forged through adversity, and perfection is achieved only when the dross is burned away, leaving behind a surface that reflects the creator's image.

In the same way the goldsmith patiently works with the gold in a room of flame, so God patiently works with us through the flames of life. However, we are not subject to the flame without purpose. In the same way the goldsmith waits until his face is reflected in the purity of the gold, so also does God use the flames of life to purify us to the point of reflecting His face. Gold having been purified is both our inheritance and His.

Thomas Watson says, "A good Christian is not like Hezekiah's sun that went backwards, nor Joshua's sun that stood still, but is always advancing in holiness, and increasing with the increase of God." If I'm honest, much of my Christian life, which extends nearly three decades now, looks a lot like Hezekiah's sun or Joshua's sun. I shared in the previous chapter a little of my story because for me, I consider it the moment I was born again. I say that loosely because yes, I believe I was previously "saved" and that if I had died, I would have been with the Lord. However, it was not until late in my twenty-fourth year of life that I would truly begin walking in my identity as His inheritance. Nearly eight years later, and I am still in the fire. Some seasons are hotter than others. Today I have stopped resisting the flame because I know that if I will allow it to accomplish His work in me, there will be no further need, for I will have been purified.

> *In this you greatly rejoice, though now for a little while you may have had to suffer grief in various trials so that the proven character of your faith—more precious than gold, which perishes even though refined by fire—may result in praise, glory, and honor at the revelation of Jesus Christ.* (1 Peter 1:6)

I have found Peter's words to be true in that I can also step back and rejoice, giving glory to God because though I'm still marble in the sculptor's hands, I can now begin to see my old, marred block taking shape into something beautiful. I say that not to boast, but I say that in humility, knowing that without the potter, I am but clay, wet and without form, fit for nothing. So, if I am to boast, it is in Him since it is in Him that I am found.

The result of grief, if it is allowed to have God's effect on us, will result in a life transformed which will bring unto Christ praise, glory, and honor. To live as Christ's inheritance is first to live in such a way that we allow the transforming work of God to be active in us, and second, it refers to the type of person we will become as a result. I am a pearl of great price, and you are too. Who you are today does not define you unless you say it does. What you've done up to this point and even those unfortunate choices you will make in the future do not define you. The thoughts which trespass involuntarily in your mind are not who you are. There is an invitation made available unto you to be someone you never thought you could be. It is an invitation to become a new creation in which the very essence of your being, down to the molecular level and the spirit, is changed.

It's not an invitation into a life of comfort and ease, but you won't find that anyway. It is, however, an invitation that will take the troubles of this world and give them meaning. It's an invitation into purpose like you've never known, and it's an invitation into a new way of living. It's an invitation into experiencing love unconditionally and into extending it freely. You can experience that "as He is so are we in this world" life as you come to find who you are and who you are invited to become through looking at Christ. When we look at Christ and we see the Father through Him, it is as though we look into a dimly lit mirror (cf. 1 Corinthians 1:31). We see Him in His Word, and His purpose for us is that we will be His image bearers, so if we see Him, we see ourselves. Yet, imagine what awaits us on the day we will no longer have a dim view but will instead stand before Him face to face.

There is now only one question that matters: "Will you accept the invitation?" The invitation not to know Him, but to first be known by Him. The more I walk alongside individuals from Christian backgrounds via counseling, the more I see a pattern emerging. Mostly everyone seems to, much like myself at one point in time, come to a conscious awareness that their theology—that is, what they know about who God is and how much scripture they know—doesn't seem to keep their anxiety or depression at bay. These things don't seem to keep them from speaking harshly to their children, and they don't seem to help them walk in humility or gentleness towards their spouse. This is a powerful crossroads because, for the first time, we begin to experientially learn that the power of the gospel isn't in our knowing but rather in our being known. We discover that while we know much truth, we have little experience with being known by God. Christ did not suffer and die to fill our heads with knowledge about Him, but to make provisions for our being intimately known by Him and consequently being loved by Him.

Will you accept the invitation?

# Category Two: Citizens

# 5. The Kingdom

*But our citizenship is in heaven, and we eagerly await a Savior from there, the Lord Jesus Christ, who, by the power that enables Him to subject all things to Himself, will transform our lowly bodies to be like His glorious body.* (Philippians 3:20-21)

To understand your identity, the gospel, and how it affects you, you must first understand that the Bible tells us the most important story in all of history. You must understand that the Bible lays out for us an account of how the world as we know it came to be, its intended purpose, and the reason you and I have our very existence. In the West, we have made the 'story of the Bible' one that centers on Jesus' work on the cross and our salvation, and rightly so. What I mean by that is if I were to ask a random churchgoer what the story of the Bible is about, the answer would most often sound something like this: "It is about the fall of humanity and Jesus' death, burial, and resurrection for our salvation from our sinful fall." All true, and highly important information, but this is merely a set of events that take place within the larger story. It would be like saying the story of Narnia is about a Lion who must die and resurrect to help save Narnia from the evil White Witch who has taken control. Well, it's true, that's a big part of the story, but it is merely a small puzzle piece that forms a much bigger picture and, perhaps more importantly, a much bigger point or purpose. The problem, however, is that this description leaves out important details that inform us as to why Aslan must die or save anything in the first place. It leaves out the fact that Narnia is a kingdom and how that kingdom came under the control of a Witch. It leaves out the fact that Aslan must overcome in partnership with four humans who are prophetic kings and queens of Narnia. You can begin to see that in much the same way, we need to view Jesus and His finished work as a series of events in a much larger story. Why did Jesus come? Why did He need to be human? What was He saving us from, or should I say unto?

> We need to view Jesus and His finished work as a series of events in a much larger story.

I digress. We've alluded previously in this book to the fact that the story of the Bible is first and foremost a story about a supreme being (God) and His desire to create and expand a kingdom on the earth. This kingdom was to be populated and governed by God's family of imager human beings. They were to begin in a Garden and eventually cover the entire earth with His kingdom, governing as divine partakers of God's very nature. This dream, however, was thwarted when Adam and Eve gave authority, through their obedience, to the divine adversary. All hope was not lost, however; the story continues with a series of events in which God unravels His plan to redeem His kingdom and His kingdom citizens.

## A 'Pilgrim' Mindset

For those who are in covenant with Christ, they are citizens not of any earthly country or kingdom, but of God's kingdom. One of America's most renowned revivalists, Vance Havner, once made the assertion, "If you are a Christian, you are not a citizen of this world trying to get to heaven; you are a citizen of heaven making your way through this world." The greatest aim of the enemy is not to get you to sin; it's to cause you to forget who you are. If he can get you to forget who you are, his aim to cause you to sin will be very easy because we are inclined to live according to how we see ourselves. In the world of psychology, the principle of 'self-concept' is a pillar. In many circles of thought, it is believed one lives according to their view of themselves by default, that is their "self-concept," even if it's subconscious. Others, like Carl Rogers, see congruence, which is the attempt to live in alignment with your self-concept, as a goal to be achieved. In either case, how you see yourself and how you define yourself directly impacts thoughts, emotions, and behaviors, thus the quickest way for the enemy to keep you from being effective as a citizen is to be successful in keeping you from realizing that you are one.

The apostles often wrote to their children in Christ to remember they are but pilgrims in the earth to live as such. The apostle Peter writes, *"Beloved, I urge you as sojourners and exiles to abstain from the passions of the flesh, which wage war against your soul."* (1 Peter 2:11, ESV) Furthermore, the apostle Paul writes:

> *These all died in faith, not having received the things promised, but having seen them and greeted them from afar, and having acknowledged that they were strangers and exiles on the earth."* (Hebrews 11:13, ESV)

Even the Psalmist recognized this critical reality of pilgrimage, *"I am a sojourner on the earth; hide not your commandments from me!"* (Psalm 119:19, ESV)

How, though, did one live as a pilgrim? First, it meant to live according to the laws, culture, and customs of the kingdom versus those of the world. We'll discuss this more below, but notice in Psalm 119:19 above that the psalmist associated God's commandments as necessary for living as a citizen on the earth. This is because God's commandments give us insight into first, who we were created to be, but also the culture, laws, and customs of His kingdom. To further illustrate, Peter connects abstaining from *"passions of the flesh"* with being a pilgrim in the earth. This is because the earth, and what comes naturally to those who live as citizens of it, is directly opposed to the culture of the kingdom. Therefore, while we are pilgrims on the earth, we are to continue living as citizens of heaven since heaven is superior to the earth and the earth is subject to it. I don't mean to get ahead of myself here, but through this, we can begin to understand heavenly authority on earth. God intends for his citizens to walk in authority, but how can they if they continually submit themselves to an inferior kingdom and way of living? If one wishes to exercise authority over demons, they must first exercise authority over themselves. The sad truth is that most of us are held captive by our daily need for coffee, while others struggle to exercise authority over a pack of Oreos, yet we wonder where the saints are who operate in a high level of kingdom authority.

The second way we live as pilgrims is by allowing our place in the kingdom to impact our earthly affairs. To illustrate, I'll get political. In America, we have an amazing freedom and opportunity that not many throughout history have had: that is the ability to vote for our leaders and to have a say in certain amendments. At the time of writing, America has just recently concluded a critical election. This election was perhaps the most critical election in history since the results would determine whether America becomes nearly unrecognizable as a nation or if we would elect leaders who promote themselves as ones who desire to get our country back on the track it was founded upon. As you can imagine, it was a tense season, but considering that the candidate who won did so with a sweeping victory, I think it's safe to say most people feel good about the direction we're now headed. During the months leading up to the election, however, our country became a divisive place. Right against the left. Conservative against liberal. It should not be this way among Kingdom citizens, however. A citizen of heaven should have an entirely different mindset regarding the election than the rest of society if they are truly allowing their identity as citizens to impact their earthly affairs.

America is a very unique place in which we are given a particular freedom, and in all reality, a luxury that the vast majority of Christians throughout history have not been so lucky to receive. In many cases, and that includes the overwhelming majority of the audience to whom the New Testament was written, the Christian community did not get a choice in their leadership, and they were subject to the ruler that was established. In many cases, the leadership was hostile towards Christians—and by hostile, I do not mean in the sense of removing their tax exemption status; I mean more along the lines of removing their heads. Nevertheless, the Christian community of Christ-following citizens was tasked with the same goal no matter if they had a leader in their favor or against their existence: that was to put on Christ. They were called to remember they were citizens of heaven first and only passing through this world that hated them. They were to remember that if the world hates them, it hated Christ first. It was their mindset that no matter who was to become leader, they were nonetheless called to live like citizens of the kingdom of heaven to which they now belong.

How does this connect, you may be wondering? Yes, let me now tie it together. An example of how a Christian living in 21st-century America during election season might allow their place in the kingdom to impact their earthly affairs is by not worrying so much about whether or not their candidate is elected. This lack of concern now frees the citizen up to no longer live as an insecure or angry American patriot who is fearful about the future of the country. It instead enables the American patriot to love those who oppose them and remain gentle and kind while perceiving a threat. If I'm an American citizen living and working from Japan during their election season, my concern for who is elected is minimal because even if a candidate who hates me is elected, I know Japan is not my home and I won't be there forever. Because I am confident in my American citizenship, I am free to not fear Japan's elected leader. I am free to live from a place of confidence rather than allowing my fears to generate unkind behaviors and attitudes of various kinds. Allowing our heavenly citizenship to govern our earthly affairs should have the same effect; it should free us from fears, stress, sadness, and anger that lead to less-than-godly behaviors.

While I encourage everyone to exercise their right to vote, it wouldn't be an alarming thing for someone to conclude that whether they did or didn't vote, or whether their preferred candidate did or didn't win, nothing changes for them except for the potential earthly comfort they might receive or lack. It is good, however, to remember earthly comfort is not owed to us and should not govern our earthly affairs. Instead, in every situation, we ought to take time and reflect upon how a kingdom citizen who is merely passing through this earth ought to think, feel, or behave in any given moment or situation.

**Citizen Mindset**

We have discussed now that a kingdom citizen allows the pilgrim mindset to govern their earthly affairs and in so doing frees themselves from an abundance of bondage. We must now discuss in brief the mindset of a citizen. A citizen, in short, lives according to the culture of their kingdom and the people to whom they belong even when they are living abroad. In the world of counseling, one thing we consider when working with those who are not native to America is how their "culturalization" process is going. This is, in essence, considering how one is adjusting to a world that is not established with their values and priorities in mind. In America, we don't make it easy for someone from a Muslim background to pray five times per day. Our work structures don't make provisions for that, we don't have giant speakers in the middle of our cities that loudly announce calls to prayer, and we don't establish our laws around their religious priorities. This is not to say someone cannot come to America and remain faithful to their Muslim culture; it just means it won't be as easy for them as it would be living in Bethlehem or Iraq.

The process of culturalization can sometimes include the process of adapting to a new culture to the point that a person drops elements of their former way of living and adjusts to the standards of their new surroundings. Sadly, many citizens in Christ do this very thing. Instead of being a citizen of heaven in a land that in many cases makes it very difficult, we can tend to undergo culturalization to the point we act like the society we're living in rather than living according to the culture of our true home. This idea begs the question, "What is the culture of heaven?"

The culture of heaven can be seen on display throughout the pages of the Bible. Cultures consist of values, laws, customs, and the overall way of doing life. It includes elements such as celebrations, traditions, vocabulary and vernacular, routine, mindsets and worldviews, and priorities, as well as food and art. Perhaps the most pertinent aspect of kingdom culture is to understand that in ancient times, kingdoms were families that expanded and took over other people groups. Therefore, the culture was often an extension of the person or people at the top. The values of the land, customs, laws, and overall way of living oftentimes were an extension of who the leadership was on an individual level. We can see this perhaps most clearly when we look at a family system. The husband and wife set the culture of the home, and it is usually based on their desires, preferences, and fundamental character as humans.

There is much of the culture of heaven that we will not have insight into until we are there or until it has come to earth in its fullness. However, for now, we can look to more deeply understand the leader of our kingdom in order to gain insights into its culture. Your homework is to read through the Bible from cover to cover with eyes specifically on the lookout for cultural attributes which I believe you'll find littered throughout the pages. For now, however, I'd like to offer the higher-level characteristics that will inform everything else. Paul writes that the matter of the kingdom is righteousness, peace, and joy (cf. Rom 14:17). In this, we see the three-chorded strand that makes up the culture of heaven and thus the character of its citizens. An entire book could be written giving in-depth attention to each of these, and perhaps it should be required reading, but for now, I will have to be content offering a brief explanation of each.

First, righteousness can be summed up as "love expressed." Righteousness is the doing of what is right and good on behalf of another. Righteousness can only be accomplished through love because love is the force that drives conduct. I have heard love defined in two ways, and I cannot choose which I prefer. First, "love is to will another's good even at your own expense." This definition aligns beautifully with the cultural trait of our people who are known by their uncanny ability to consider others as more important than themselves. Second, "love is to do what you don't want to do when you don't want to do it, for the benefit of another while keeping a good attitude." My father, when I was young, would drive me to school and tell me every day that discipline was "doing what you don't want to do when you don't want to do it, so you can have what you want when you want it." It recently clicked for me; love is a discipline. Perhaps more importantly, love is an action requiring discipline, and the Bible defines the action birthed from love as righteousness. If we will then love our fellow man and ourselves, we will walk in righteousness.

The culture of our kingdom is also peace. In saying this, I must be clear that peace is not just the feeling or state of being one experiences when adversity is absent. Peace is often a choice and must be created or chosen. When Paul writes that we ought to let the peace of Christ rule in our hearts (cf. Col 3:15), he is not talking about the emotion. He is teaching us that we should allow Christ's peace to govern our decisions, desires, and motives. The picture of Abraham and Lot comes to mind here. In Genesis, we see a moment in the narrative when Abraham and Lot were faced with a dilemma: their herds and hired servants grew too big to coexist. Therefore, to ease the hostility and to keep peace in the family, Abraham, who had the right to send Lot on his way, appeals to Lot and tells him to pick for himself which of the property he would take as his own. Whatever was left, Abraham would go and settle on. Lot, of course, chose the fertile land, and because Abraham valued peace in his relationship with Lot, he humbly accepted the unfertile land. The peace of Christ led Abraham to consider Lot as more important than himself to the point of giving up what was rightfully his and moving to a less desirable piece of land all to maintain peace and harmony between families.

With that being said, peace is also a state of being that we have access to in Christ. It is, however, not the absence of adversity. Jesus tells us in this world we will have trouble, but then he tells us to 'take heart'; one could argue this means 'be at peace,' for He overcame the world. What is Jesus saying here? In essence, he is saying that peace isn't defined by the absence of storms but rather by the ability to sleep in the midst of them. Because Christ overcame, we can now have an abundant life in the midst of a broken world.

This leads us to joy. It is a topic thoroughly written on by many of Christianity's great thinkers throughout time. C.S. Lewis famously described joy as a signpost pointing to something beyond this world. In *Confessions*, Augustine of Hippo described how the human heart is restless until it rests in God, and joy is the result of finding satisfaction in Him. This aligns with J.I. Packer's statement, "Joy is at the heart of satisfied living."

*The* INVITATION

Dietrich Bonhoeffer and other thinkers have noted that joy rooted in Christ is not diminished by trials but can even grow through them, showing us that joy is not inferior to suffering. However, there is something that can rob us of our joy, and that is fear. R.C. Sproul once said, "It is anxiety that robs us of our joy. And what is anxiety but fear? Fear is the enemy of joy. It is hard to be joyful when we are afraid." But let me be clear here: fear is not superior to joy, for if one chooses to be joyful, fear cannot remain. A.W. Tozer so appropriately notes that "Joy is a great therapeutic for the mind."

Since joy is a cultural pillar in our kingdom, we have a solution to fear and suffering. The path to a life of joy is first found in proximity to the king. The world should know a kingdom citizen by their ability to be joyful in the midst of stress, suffering, fear, and dare I even say, trauma.

Citizens of the Kingdom should be easily identified by their actions and attitude. I was recently told that in Japanese employees do something quite opposite of western employees. I was told that in Japan those who arrive to work early will park farther away from the entrance in efforts to make it easier on those running late. This cultural custom comes from a place of mutual respect. How true this is, I do not know, but it illustrates well for us how culture should identify us. We must bear in mind that Christ said we will be identified by our fruit. The three fruits mentioned here are how citizens should be identified in a land that looks entirely different. In the carnal world, we consider ourselves as more important than others. "Look out for number one," they say. In this carnal world, we allow our emotions of stress, anxiety, and rage to govern our actions and rule our hearts. In this world, our sufferings make us melancholy and, in many cases, selfish. However, as a citizen, it is the culture of our land to love in selflessness, choose peace in conflict, and have joy in suffering. Let's move forward now and discover what it means to be a citizen and how it connects to an ecclesia, for I am convinced it is not what we think.

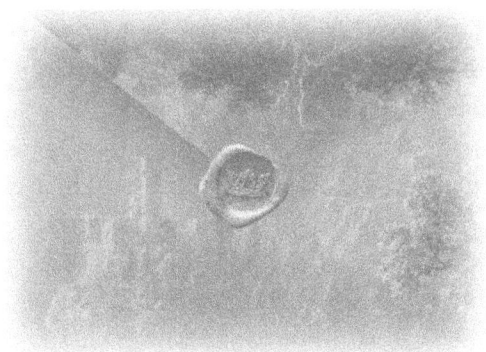

# 6. The True Ecclesia

*"On this rock I will build My <u>ecclesia</u>, and the gates of Hades will not prevail against it."* - Jesus

Believe it or not, in order for one to grasp with any sense of accuracy their identity as a citizen in God's kingdom, they must first understand what an ecclesia is because, as you will see, the ecclesia is to a citizen as a courtroom is to a jury. You cannot separate the two, and just as a courtroom informs us of what a jury's purpose is, so does an ecclesia in its proper historical context inform us of what a citizen is and how that translates to our role as citizens in the ecclesia Jesus is building.

I'll unpack this daring statement that I'm about to make later in this chapter, but you must, from the very beginning, understand that **the ecclesia is not a church**. Jesus is not saying that he is going to build a local church as we think of it today. Now, before you close the book prematurely, let me put your mind at ease. I am not one of those who are anti-gathering or anti-local church. On the contrary, as you'll see, I think there is quite the need for those and one that is rooted in scripture. However, what I am suggesting is that the ecclesia and the local church are not the same but rather distinct, and the proper understanding of both will in turn create not just free saints in Christ but powerful saints who walk in and use their kingdom authority to bind and loose on earth as in heaven. I am convinced that a core contributor to the state of powerless Christianity running rampant in our world today is the successful campaign of the enemy to blind people to what it means to be a citizen and a member of the ecclesia. So, let's begin.

**The Gospel Jesus Preached**

First, a quick refresher. What is the gospel Jesus preached? If you recall from the previous chapter, the story of the Bible is about a kingdom. Notice the gospel Jesus preached was not the gospel of "I'm here to die for your sins so you can go to heaven." The gospel Jesus preached was the gospel of the kingdom.

> *From that time on Jesus began to preach, 'Repent, for <u>the kingdom</u> of heaven is near...Jesus went throughout Galilee, teaching in their synagogues, preaching the gospel of the kingdom, and healing every disease and sickness among the people.'"* (Matt 4:17, 23)

The kingdom is the central focus of conversation or teaching; it is mentioned at least 119 times in the gospels alone. The central message has always been about a kingdom; it's not about religion. With that being said, I need to be clear that the intent here is not to minimize the life, death, and resurrection of Christ. It is central to the story. However, what we should begin to see is that over the last +/- 1500 years, the church has majored in a message that

Jesus, the apostles, and first-century followers minored in. As we've discussed, that message is the gospel of "going to heaven." In essence, it's a reduction of the gospel to "Jesus died for our sins so that we could go to heaven," or, if we're being honest, for many it's more about avoiding hell. But what does this message even mean? Simply stated, it's an attempt to say that "sin cannot inherit God's kingdom and He wants you in His kingdom, so he had to deal with your sin."

This begs the question though, "What is sin?" In a simplified response, sin means to "miss the mark," but it doesn't primarily refer to wrongdoing. The term "sin" actually refers more to the essence of one's nature. One does ungodly things because quite simply they are not like God. **To miss the mark is to not be His image bearer; it is to miss the mark of Godlikeness.** The ungodly deeds that we tend to classify as 'sin' are indeed sin but only because we are first the *type of people* who would conduct ourselves in a manner unlike God. To be in sin is to be human when we were created to be holy (like God). Therefore, to enable us to enter His kingdom, He had to restore us back into His image so that we might become partakers of His divine nature (2 Peter 1:4). This is accomplished through faith and sanctification, which is the process of being transformed into His image (2 Thessalonians 2:13).

While the most popular rendering of the gospel is truly good news, it is merely the tip of the iceberg, but the problem with making the tip of an iceberg the central focus is the vast majority is left under the surface and, if not considered, can sink the ship. Allow me to present an example. One danger in making "getting into heaven" our sole focus is that we begin to create a bunch of selfish converts who actually just "get saved" for selfish reasons, i.e., to avoid hell. Did you know your faith in Jesus could be more motivated by loyalty to yourself than to King Jesus? If all we understand the gospel to be is a claim that if you "believe in Jesus when you die you won't be in eternal torment," then we will create people who get "saved" for themselves and never actually learn to live holy, authoritative lives, full of power and freedom before they die. It is so easy to make our faith about "what Jesus can do for me." We pray prayers like, "Jesus save me, heal me, bless me, open up opportunities, meet my emotional needs", and so on. Before we know it, we are led to think of God as more of a genie than a king.

A second danger, and perhaps the more detrimental of the two, is that we can emphasize a gospel that strips us of our authority in Christ as citizens because it never teaches us who we are in Christ, which is the heart behind this book. It shouldn't come as a surprise to you to know Jesus wasn't concerned with forming a religion, and the Bible isn't primarily a religious textbook, though many would try to reduce it down to that.

The major foundation that I need for you to understand is that the entire Bible is a library of books documenting the true story of a Kingdom that was birthed but compromised before it expanded. Then through Israel, the kingdom was reconstructed as a temporary and watered-down replica (shadow), until finally it could be re-birthed (through Christ) and will eventually be expanded when He returns to set up His government. With that foundation laid, let's move forward.

**Our Foundational Text**

> *"But you," he asked them, "who do you say that I am?" Simon Peter answered, "You are the Messiah, the Son of the living God." Jesus responded, "Blessed are you, Simon son of Jonah, because flesh and blood did not reveal this to you, but my Father in heaven. And I also say to you that you are Peter, and on this rock, I will build my church, and the gates of Hades will not overpower it. I will give you the keys of the kingdom of heaven, and whatever you bind on earth will have been bound in heaven, and whatever you loose on earth will have been loosed in heaven." Then he gave the disciples orders to tell no one that he was the Messiah.* Matthew 16:15-20.

There are several observations we need to extract from this text before moving forward. First, when Peter identifies Jesus as the Messiah, this was not a claim to divinity. Peter eventually did come to recognize Jesus as God in the flesh; however, that is not what the messiah insinuates. The idea Peter had in mind for the messiah was, in essence, a king who would set up a government in Israel that would last forever and lead the way in world peace. This is important because by recognizing what's in Peter's mind, we are able to see the story is again about a kingdom being established. The text goes on, and Jesus famously claims he will build his ecclesia. (Just wait until we unpack what the ecclesia is, later on; it's wild!) Finally, he says he will distribute the keys to the kingdom, and with those keys, his members of the ecclesia (called 'citizens' as we'll soon discover) would bind and loose things on earth as they are in heaven, and as a result of this authority, the gates of hades would not be able to prevail. Notice this passage is about a kingdom going to war with another kingdom. It is about the citizens of one kingdom redeeming territory from another kingdom. That "territory" is here, at this moment, on this physical earth. Jesus is not talking about a spiritual warfare that is far-off in space and time.

**Linguistic Insights**

In linguistics and when interpreting foreign languages, there are three things I need you to know about. First, we have translation, which most of us know quite well how that works. 'Hola' translated from Spanish to English is 'Hello.' The vast majority of the Bible is translated from Hebrew, Greek, and in some cases Aramaic into English. Second, there is a technique called transliteration, which is the act of assigning English letters to a foreign word so that it can be pronounced but not translated. For example, the word Nephilim is a transliteration from the Hebrew text. Nephilim is a Hebrew word that was given English letters so that we may pronounce it in Hebrew. A translation of Nephilim is 'giant.' Finally, we have loan words, which are when foreign words are taken and sometimes adjusted slightly to create new words; they are, in essence, borrowed words. For instance, 'amen' is a loan word that comes from Hebrew, and it means "let it be" or "certainly." Likewise, 'kindergarten' is a loan word from the German language which means "children's garden." Finally, the word 'angel' is actually a form of loan word from the Greek term 'angelos' which just means "messenger."

Why is that relevant, you might ask? Because the word 'church' used for ecclesia is neither a translation, transliteration, nor loan word. Many mistakenly assume that the term 'church' is a translation of ecclesia, but in fact, it is not. The most accepted translation for ecclesia is "called out ones," and this, of course, has nothing to do with what we think of as a church gathering. The term 'church', many believe, has its connections back to the Greek term "kyriakon (kear-ee-a-kōn) doma" meaning "the Lord's house." Here's my bold claim; are you ready?

> The word 'church' used for ecclesia is neither a translation, transliteration, nor loan word.

**The English term "church" and what it is, especially today in our world, is not what an ecclesia was. It arguably does not fit in our Bibles where the word ecclesia is used.**

The reason we do not have an English word to translate ecclesia to is that, simply put, we do not have an ecclesia in our society. Now, some translate ecclesia as an "assembly," and this is a lot closer but still too ambiguous because the ecclesia wasn't merely an assembly; however, the ecclesia did assemble in order to accomplish their purpose. Furthermore, the term ecclesia does not denote the gathering of a body of Christians to worship or study God's word. There is a specific Greek word for that called "episunagoge" {epi-synago-ay}. The apostle

*The* INVITATION

Paul writes, *"Let us not neglect the gathering together…."* (Hebrews 10:25) **To the first-century audience, referring to the ecclesia as a church would be equivalent to us referring to congress as a church just because they congregate.** No, the ecclesia was a position, and it had a very specific role and function.

**Athens, the Origins of the Ecclesia**

Now after reading these words from Jesus, we need to be asking the questions. First, what is an ecclesia as the original hearers would have known it? Secondly, what does it have to do with taking down the gates of hell? And finally, what does it have to do with binding and loosing on earth as in heaven? To understand what an ecclesia is and the answer to these questions, we need to know a little bit about ancient Athens' democratic system since that is where it derived, and elements of it were adopted by Rome in the first century period in which Jesus lived. Remember that we are dealing with the Greco-Roman world as we read the gospels and much of the New Testament epistles.

To begin, both ancient Israel, as we read about throughout the Old Testament, and Athens had classes of residents. There was the 'foreign resident,' which are sometimes referred to as 'resident aliens' in the Old Testament. These were people who had no blood connection to the people of the country they now lived in, yet they went through the proper protocol to become legal residents of the nation. Next, there were 'slaves'; these were not the type of slaves that are thought of in connection to the civil rights era in America. To be more precise, these were the working-class residents who often had outstanding debt that they couldn't pay. If you're interested, head over to Joshua chapter nine and read about the Gibeonites. This chapter gives an account of how people became slaves and what their role was.

From here we have what I refer to as 'residents of blood descent.' This class consisted of those whose mother and father were both blood residents of the nation in which they reside. In Athens, this means both the mother and father must be Athenian by blood. Finally, there was a very special class of residents known as 'citizens.' Citizens consisted of only men over the age of 20 who belonged to parents who were Athenian by blood. You can see how it differs from our Western mindset where a 'citizen' is anyone with legal residence. The term citizen mentioned throughout scripture, which is in reference to those in Christ, does not just mean we have legal residency in heaven, though it includes that. Citizenship in heaven means something so much better.

In Athenian culture, the ecclesia only consisted of residents who were citizens. No one else was permitted to be a part of the ecclesia nor fulfill their role. This system was not original to Athens, however. It would seem that God's original system of government included this feature. It worked similarly in Israel long before Athens was formed. Throughout the Old Testament and especially throughout Exodus-Deuteronomy, we can see an ecclesia at work. For example, in Israel, you had to be a Jew, which is a blood descendant of Jacob, or you were considered a gentile and at best a resident alien.

The ecclesia was the **central political institution of the state**. The members of the ecclesia were not elected but joined the assembly by right as they wished. They were called out to meet as an assembly in a specific meeting hall within the city where they would meet and discuss matters related to the kingdom. The ecclesia were citizens, that is, men over twenty who had a mother and father of Athenian blood, who were called out to assemble for the purpose of deciding on matters such as "laws, treaties, decrees, or to go to war." The Greek-English Lexicon of the New Testament defines ecclesia this way: "the ecclesia was a regularly summoned <u>legislative</u> body." Notice they were not a regularly summoned religious body, yet sadly that is what it has become in most of the earth today. The difference is one advances their kingdom while the other simply talks about the kingdom.

Therefore, with all this in mind, it is now easier to see that when Jesus said he was building an ecclesia, He had in mind the Athenian ecclesia as it pertained to a governmental system designed for ruling and reigning. The amazing news, however, is everyone, and by that, I do mean everyone, is invited to be not just residents in His kingdom but to be citizens, and as citizens, members of his legislative and governing leadership known as the ecclesia! But wait, there's more. If you thought it couldn't get any better, you should know that your ruling and reigning with Christ starts not when you've died and been resurrected, but rather it begins now.

My friend, this life is training for reigning.

**The Gospel According to Paul**

Here's a snapshot of the gospel as laid out by Paul: First, we are all grafted into "blood resident status" through Abraham since the seed from which we must be born again is a seed of faith, not a seed of blood (Galatians 3:7). Therefore, when we are born again, we become God's very descendants. Since God is spirit, not flesh and blood, when we are born from His seed, we become direct relatives. Additionally, not only are we blood residents through being born of faith and by the Spirit (John 3), but we are also citizens because, *"There is neither male nor female, Jew nor Greek, slave or free since you are all one in Christ Jesus."* (Galatians 3:28) Lastly, Jesus tore down the dividing wall of hostility: *"For he is our peace, who made both groups, that is Jew and Gentile, one and tore down the dividing wall of hostility."* (Ephesians 2:14)

On the temple mount in Jerusalem, there were layers such as the inner court, outer court, holy of holies, and so on. Each of these layers progressed, and the closer one got to the holy of holies, the fewer people were permitted. In one of the final three layers, there was a short wall about knee or waste height, and this wall marked the furthest a gentile male could go in the temple. From the dividing wall forward, only Jewish males could proceed. In Christ, this dividing wall has been destroyed, and there are no longer classes of residents to whom access to the Father's presence is restricted or limited. Now, all are considered citizens and relatives of the King. This is the gospel, at least a much fuller treatment of it that is often left out or at best under-emphasized in our society today.

> Now, all are considered citizens and relatives of the King.

As powerful as the information we've unpacked in this chapter is, it is of minimal use if we do not know how to apply it to our lives. Therefore, the content we've just discussed leads us to a series of further questions. How then should we act as citizens and members of this legislative body called the ecclesia? What do we do and what is our role? In what ways should we utilize this newfound authority in Christ? What are 'binding' and 'loosing,' and how do we operate in such a manner as to remove the gates of Hades?

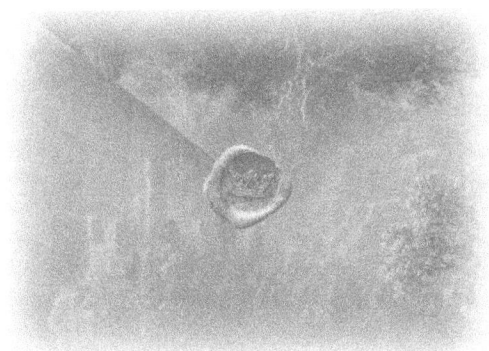

# 7. Three Dimensions of Citizenship

*"The world's idea of greatness is to rule, but Christian greatness consists in serving."* - John Charles Ryle (Bishop of Liverpool)

*"God's compassion is a compassion that reveals itself in servanthood."* - Donald McNeill

In conclusion of this section on our identity as a kingdom citizen in Christ's ecclesia, I'd like to lay out a few ways in which we fulfill our role in advancing the kingdom, since after all, that was the objective of a citizen when taking their place in the local ecclesia. I'd like to keep this chapter brief because some of what we'll cover here is unpacked in more depth in the other sections throughout the book. To avoid redundancy, I will try my best to keep the content in this chapter more generalized and less elucidated.

Being a kingdom citizen involves three broad dimensions. Of course, there are more that exist for those of you who'd like to think further on the subject. These three are not my attempt to consolidate all the nuances into an inclusive list; rather, these three are broad brush strokes that should provide us with a good idea of the dimensions of being a kingdom citizen. The first dimension is responsibility, the second is service, and the third is authority. In this chapter, we will cover each of these in brief as well as attempt to touch on five key areas of service or 'roles' that a citizen may assume that are designed to advance the kingdom when operating in cohesion.

**What is the Kingdom of God?**

Before any of that, however, we must come to a common understanding of what the Kingdom of Heaven is and what it is not. If we have improper thinking towards the kingdom, it will inevitably lead to an improper functioning within the kingdom; and yes, the kingdom as well as our involvement in it has already begun. This claim, I understand, finds itself contrary to the long-held and popular idea that the kingdom is a place 'saved' folk enter upon their death, or for some, upon the dawning of the new age. My favorite philosopher, Dallas Willard, whom I have not quoted nearly enough in this book, defines the Kingdom of God so beautifully. He describes it this way, "The Kingdom of God is the range of God's effective will. It is where what He wants done is done."

A kingdom is an area in which a king has dominion and what He wants done is done. Now, we must see that each of us in fact has our own kingdom. It is precisely where our will is enacted by invoking our will into a situation and thus exercising dominion. The kingdom of heaven is not primarily a place we go once we die. The gospel story concludes with a new earth in which God's kingdom (i.e., the area of His domain) is set up and we rule and reign with Him 'here,' not 'there.' Jesus teaches that His kingdom is in fact at hand, which is to say that it is available now, at least to some capacity. Those of us who would dare seek it can access it and establish it here on earth as it is in heaven. Seeking the Kingdom simply put is seeking the effective will of the king to be done in your sphere of existence. This requires, however, that we do something with our personal kingdom because no kingdom can have two kings each trying to exercise dominion. It is precisely at this crossroads that we learn what Jesus means when he says "Nevertheless, let not my will be done but yours." Our will, that is our intentions, must be subordinated to God's if we are to operate in His kingdom. This is of the utmost importance because we can only walk as a citizen in the kingdom we are a citizen of. Therefore, the first bridge we must cross, so far as it pertains to walking as an authoritative citizen, is simply coming to terms with whose kingdom we are operating from at any given moment. Whose dominion are you carrying forth into your sphere of existence? Now, the effect of this is that one must ask the question "What is the will of God and how does one live in it?" That is in large part a goal of discipleship which we will address in more depth later.

## The 'Will' vs. 'Desire'

Before moving forward, I'd like to bring forth one more distinction, and that is we must understand that 'will' and 'desire' are not the same. Allow me to illustrate what I mean. Let's imagine I encounter a man in public who is quite insolent and has an uncivil episode in which I am the primary beneficiary of harm. Let's imagine that the man acts selfishly so as to benefit himself and cost me a great deal of time, money, and emotional energy. Fast forward now, it is a month or two later and while I am out in town, I see this same man walking along the street with a sign that reads "Recently unemployed. Wife and child at home, please help." If I can be honest, in that moment I am likely not going to *desire* to help the man by giving him my hard-earned money. I am probably not going to *desire* to turn my car around and spend my valuable time and energy buying him groceries or a gift card. If I'm being honest, I'll probably more than likely desire him to suffer a little longer so as to learn not to treat people the way he treated me a while back. However, while I may 'feel' this way or 'desire' these things inwardly, I simultaneously have a unique set of intentions and a "will" to do the very things I do not desire to do. These intentions are informed by my maturation as a citizen. As I learn the will of the king over time, I become responsible and accountable for whether or not I choose to implement it, thus expanding the effective range in which what He wants done is done. To conclude, the will is the thing we have the intention to carry out, not the thing we feel like or "desire" to carry out. Willard again says it so well

> Individually the disciple and friend of Jesus who has learned to work shoulder to shoulder with his or her Lord stands in this world as a point of contact between heaven and earth, a kind of Jacob's ladder by which the angels of God may ascend from and descend into human life. Thus, the disciple stands as an envoy or a

## Dimension of Responsibility

Kingdom citizenship calls for a lifestyle of responsibility, where citizens reflect the values of God's Kingdom in their daily lives. Our sphere of responsibility can be summed up in two broad categories; we are responsible to God and to others. I know for some it might be less than appealing, but it shouldn't feel daunting to hear that we are responsible to God and to others. When we focus on being responsible to God, we will simultaneously meet our responsibilities to others. There is but one thing God asks of us and that is to mature in love. In Matthew, we read that "Jesus declared

> "**Love** the Lord your God with all your heart and with all your soul and with all your mind." This is the first and greatest commandment. And the second is like it: "**Lov**e your neighbor as yourself." All the Law and the Prophets hang on these two commandments. (Matthew 22:37-40, Mark 12:31)

Paul also teaches the Galatians, "The entire law is fulfilled in a single decree: '**Love** your neighbor as yourself.'" (Galatians 5:14) And again he teaches the church in Rome:

> The commandments "Do not commit adultery," "Do not murder," "Do not steal," "Do not covet," and **any other commandments, are summed up in this one decree**: "Love your neighbor as yourself." Love does no wrong to its neighbor. Therefore, love is the fulfillment of the law. (Romans 13:9-10)

*The* INVITATION

If we remember our working definitions of love to "will" or "intend" the good of another, then we begin to gain a clearer picture of what it is God asks of us and how we expand His kingdom on the earth. Jesus' words in the gospel of John begin to make much more sense when He says, *"If you love Me, you will keep My commandments."* (John 14:15) It is to say, "If you intend my good you will keep my commandments which are to intend the Father's good (and glory) and to intend the good of His creation."

To love is our primary responsibility to God and to others. Of course, there is much depth and nuance that can be unpacked here. For instance, we could bridge now into our responsibility to God in walking holy and living righteously. The apostle Peter reminds his audience of God's command, *"For it is written: 'Be holy because I am holy.'"* (1 Peter 1:16) And again, Paul reminds us in his letter to the Corinthians that the purpose of our lives is to glorify the Father, *"Therefore glorify God with your body."* (1 Corinthians 6:20) These are extensions and expressions of love.

How then are we responsible for others? Yes, we are tasked with loving them, but let us be more specific for a moment. What are some ways in which we are responsible for loving others as kingdom citizens? First, we mustn't overlook the fundamental truth that before we can love others by doing something for them, we must first love others by becoming a particular type of person. In Micah 6:8, the prophet delivers God's command, *"What does the LORD require of you but to act justly, to love mercy, and to walk humbly with your God?"* If we are not careful, we will be tempted to read God's commands as **things to do**, and if we fail to do them, then we will be met with some

## Three Dimensions of Citizenship

sort of consequence. However, that's a dangerous way to interpret scripture or God's actual desires for us.

There are two ways I can interpret God's words to Micah. First, I could read them as they most naturally sound, like commands. Do justice, be merciful, be humble, and walk with God all day every day as though we must be a saint resigned to monastery life and taken out of the 'real world.' Unfortunately, most people will come away with an interpretation that is not too far off.

The second way it could be interpreted, and I would assert that it should be interpreted this way, is to "be a just person who naturally acts justly, be a merciful and forgiving person who would find it harder to hold offense than to extend mercy, and be a person of humility that desires to walk closely with God in the real world for the purpose of revealing Him to a world who is in need of Him."

I know there is a lot of extra theology packed into that second interpretation, but what I want you to come away with is this: God desires you to not just act justly but to be the type of person for whom justice is natural. He does not desire you to be merciful but rather that you be the type of person from whom mercy freely flows. He has no intention of burdening you with commands that you in your nature cannot carry out. His purpose for laying out these commands is to reveal to us the type of people we are and the type of people we are not. Through these commands,

He shows us who He is and the type of people we were created to be in the Garden as His imagers.

Today, as fallen humans, it is utterly futile to *try* and be humble. We can't do it in our own strength. It is utterly pointless to *try* to be merciful, kind, gentle, or generous, and yet, we are called to *"make every effort"* to add to our faith virtue (1 Peter 2:5-8). How can that be? These things do not require *trying*; they depend on *training*, for Paul says, *"Everyone who competes in the games trains with strict discipline."* (1 Corinthians 9:25) But that is a discussion for another time. We, on our own, cannot do it. We must be transformed, that is, regenerated, by His Spirit, and from then on, any fruit we produce in His likeness is by only His Grace working in us.

From this foundation, we can then name a myriad of specific traits or actions we should conduct ourselves in as citizens releasing God's domain and will in the earth. We are responsible to forgive others when they have trespassed against us. It goes without saying, but this issue is quite imperative to our own well-being and freedom. Yet, more than forgiving, we are to be the type of people who find it harder to hold offense than to forgive. I imagine Jesus on the cross as he is pouring out sweat and blood. He is no doubt utilizing any ounce of moisture He can gather from his saliva to satisfy the dryness in his mouth, all the while grasping for air. I wonder how difficult it must have been to forgive his murderers on his final breath. However, when I think about it, I am forced to conclude that no matter how hard it must have been to forgive, it would have been much harder for Jesus to hold an offense against them. He was simply the kind of person who could not withhold mercy.

## Three Dimensions of Citizenship

We are also responsible for considering others as more important than ourselves and doing all things without grumbling and complaining (Philippians 2:3,14). However, the same principles apply here as they do to our previously mentioned traits. These are not merely commands, but rather descriptions reminding us what kind of being God is and equally what kind of beings we ought to be as His imagers in the earth.

### Dimension of Service

Service is central to Kingdom citizenship, modeled after Jesus, who came not to be served but to serve. Kingdom citizens are called to emulate Christ by serving others selflessly and with humility. Paul teaches the church in Philippians the importance of this dimension using Christ as the model:

> *Do nothing out of selfish ambition or empty pride, but in humility consider others more important than yourselves. Each of you should look not only to your own interests but also to the interests of others. Let this mind be in you which was also in Christ Jesus: Who existing in the form of God, did not consider equality with God something to be grasped but emptied Himself, taking the form of a servant."* (Philippians 2:3-7)

When we serve in this manner, considering others as more important than ourselves, we use our authority to release light from our kingdom into the darkness of the kingdom established in the earth.

I have had the honor to work with many marriages up to this point, and a common denominator that is true among all of them is that somewhere along the line they have stopped serving and they have started grumbling. They have both begun trying to extend the range of their effective will and establish their kingdom, and it has led to the battle between two kingdoms. They have begun living opposite to the nature of the kingdom, and yet they wonder why God's blessings seem so very distant from their home. It is not because God is punishing them or has distanced Himself; it is because they are using their authority to establish the dominion of a kingdom that does not carry with it the blessings that they seek. In conclusion of this dimension, I'd like to leave you with a thought. What would it look like if we, the citizens of the kingdom, tried to out-serve one another? What would it look like if we got just as competitive about serving as we do our sports, video games, or trivia? How different might our spheres of existence be?

> What would it look like if we, the citizens of the kingdom, tried to out-serve one another?

**Dimension of Authority**

Kingdom citizenship also grants us authority, which comes from Christ, the King, and empowers citizens to act in alignment with God's purposes. What does it mean to be given the *"keys to the kingdom"* and to 'bind' and 'loose' other than to possess and exercise authority? As citizens, we are to be advancing the kingdom in such a manner that the *"gates of hell cannot prevail against it."* In this, we see our first sphere of authority as citizens is over darkness. This, to be clear, does not mean we go out and start challenging demonic powers and principalities to epic duals. Though the realms of spiritual warfare may include casting out demons, it is not the most immediate or even important use of our authority. The kingdom of darkness has taken dominion over the earth, and God, who sits enthroned over the kingdom of light, has initiated war on the kingdom of darkness. The Father intends to take over the land in which darkness has established its dominance. This is why the 'gates' of hell will not stand.

Notice that gates are defensive in nature, which means we, the citizens of the kingdom of light, are to be on the offensive. We are to *"go therefore and make disciples of all nations."* The light we carry has authority to overthrow the darkness and when overthrown, the kingdom of God will be established. When we take the effective will of the king into an area where His effective will is not enacted, we in essence use our authority as citizens to expand the King's domain and take down strongholds where hell once had gates established in the hearts, minds, and emotions of those around us. Our authority is first and foremost utilized in our own light bearing, for when we bear our light, we act as an ambassador making decisions on behalf of our country and king while residing in a foreign land. As ambassadors (2 Corinthians 5:20), we carry the responsibility of representing God's rule and reign wherever we go. This includes declaring God's truth, living as examples of Kingdom values, and bringing about God's will on earth as it is in heaven (Matthew 6:10).

**Conclusion on the Five-Fold**

In conclusion, I must touch on the importance of the five-fold ministry outlined by Paul. If the English word 'church' in our Bible is no longer something I can think of as a weekly religious gathering but rather a gathering of citizens with legislative authority, I need to re-think how the five-fold offices play into the true ecclesia. This idea could be fleshed out in a book of its own but briefly, I'd like to give a brief overview of the purpose of each role so that you may begin to rethink how their function might be applicable not in a religious setting but in a setting in which we are all active members in the expansion campaign of God's kingdom of light in a world dominated by darkness.

Paul lays out five offices: the apostle, prophet, pastor, teacher, and evangelist. The apostle refers to those who are sent out by Christ to speak and act with special authority. In many cases, this individual was responsible for going into new or hostile territory and proclaiming a King's message that would have challenged the way of living or thinking of a community. A special degree of authority was given to the apostles because of the special nature, risk, and weight of the assignment that they were sent to accomplish. In some sense, we all act as apostles, but I won't get into that here. A prophet refers to those who are designated by God to speak on His behalf. Again, in some sense, we may all speak on God's behalf, but that does not mean we operate under the function of a prophet. A prophet most often calls a people to repentance, and in an Old Testament sense, the prophet was a mouthpiece between God and humanity (most often His citizens, Israel). An evangelist refers to those who proclaim the truth of the gospel and call others to live by Jesus' standards. In contrast to a prophet, the evangelist tends to be the bearer of 'good news' rather than judgment or futuristic events. A pastor refers to those who care for or protect the citizens of God's kingdom. Since the Greek word used here, poimēn, literally means "shepherd" and is often translated as such, this role corresponds with the New Testament portrayal of the Church as God's flock. Often pastors make the best counselors, and they are most often a natural fit for this service. Today, we (protestants) tend to slap the title pastor onto every position in the local church, and I am of the opinion that this is a practice that has led to the confusion of church roles and offices and perhaps even contributed to the deterioration of the five-fold functioning in a healthy manner in our local congregations. Finally, we have teachers. A teacher indicates those who faithfully pass on the teachings of a king or kingdom, especially through explaining, applying, but perhaps most importantly through modeling.

It's important to know how each of these roles plays out in a local congregation but also in the active participation of kingdom expansion. An ecclesia in ancient Athens would gather, yes, but no real advancement to the kingdom took place in the gathering. It was what the citizens did and how they functioned according to their authority and offices *after the meeting concluded* that led to kingdom advancement. It is much the same with the Kingdom of Heaven. For further study on the five-fold, see: Titus 2:1, 1 Peter 5:2, Acts 20:28, Acts 21:8, 2 Tim 4:5, Ephesians 2:20, 1 Corinthians 12:10.

*The* INVITATION

William Gurnall once said:

> The sincere Christian is progressive—never at his journey's end till he gets to heaven. This keeps him always in motion, advancing in his desires and endeavors forward.

It's important to remember that learning our identity, growing as citizens, and maturing into light-producing fruit bearers takes time and training. It is a journey, and the goal is not speed but endurance. Let us move forward now into discussing God's plan for expanding His kingdom on the earth and His plan for training and equipping future generations of kingdom citizens by discussing a strategy and system called discipleship.

# Category Three: Disciples

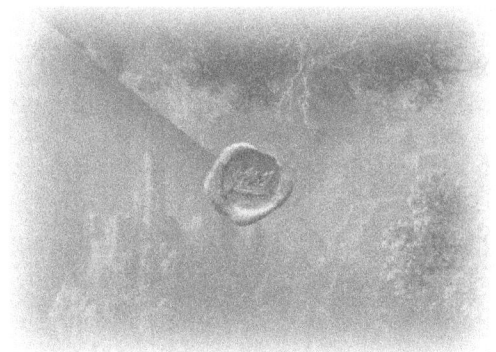

# 8. A Vision for Becoming

*"Christianity without discipleship is always Christianity without Christ."* - Dietrich Bonhoeffer

*"Discipleship is the process of becoming who Jesus would be if he were you."* – Dallas Willard

*"A true disciple is not just a student or a learner, but a follower: one who applies what he has learned."* – Rev Stan Smith

To be a disciple of Christ comes at a great cost, yes, but I'd like to just point out that not being a disciple of Christ equally comes at a great cost. If you are not a disciple of Christ, then what are you a disciple of, for we are all being formed (the result of discipleship) into a particular type of person? Both Ted Bundy and Corrie Ten Boom equally underwent discipleship and a process of spiritual formation even if they were unaware. We are disciples of something, that is, we are being formed and shaped into a particular type of person by something or someone no matter if we intentionally choose it or remain oblivious to it. If you're reading this chapter, it's likely that at a minimum you're fairly interested in what it practically requires to walk in the identity of Christ's disciple.

Before diving into the practicalities, I must make a couple of disclaimers. First, discipleship to Christ, contrary to many heresies circulating today, is not a path of promised prosperity or blessings, at least in the earthly or material sense. However, it does come with an abundance of blessings in other ways. Further, it is not a choice that guarantees us an easy path, but it does guarantee us an easy yoke. Jesus makes two important claims regarding being his disciple. First, that *"In this world, you will have trouble."* And second, *"My yoke is easy, and my burden is light."* I love what William Barclay says about the matter in his commentary on the Gospel of Luke. "Jesus promised his disciples three things—that they would be completely fearless, absurdly happy, and in constant trouble." Nevertheless, I'd rather be in constant trouble as a disciple of Jesus than in constant trouble apart from Him, so onward we go!

**Proper Thinking Regarding Discipleship**

Discipleship is a complicated subject for many people because they easily grow conflicted by the way discipleship is often presented. Discipleship by nature is something we first intend to do and then apply effort to do. It most often involves discipline and training. Yet, our salvation is supposed to be by grace alone through faith alone, and not of works; therefore, suggesting discipleship as essential to being a Christian creates an understandable hesitancy. Willard makes an important distinction and that is that Grace is opposed to earning, not to effort. We cannot earn our salvation through our effort, nor can we earn our salvation through the level of maturity we attain. Salvation is a gift and any level of maturation we achieve is also a gift. This chapter must be established upon Paul's words to the Philippian church, *"For it is God who works in you to will and to act on behalf of His good purpose."* (Philippians 2:13) God will not override the free will He gave us so that He may force us to follow Christ into His way of living from the Kingdom towards the earth, but if we choose to seek and follow, He will then do what we cannot do on our own, namely, He will give us the will, desire, and ability to *act*, (i.e., produce fruit) in this life. In the end, though we apply effort, discipline, and training, it is still God's Grace freely extended unto which produces the fruit. It is imperative that before addressing the practicalities of discipleship we grasp these truths lest we enter into bondage in our well-meaning attempt to walk in our identity as a disciple. The enemy has long used the good intentions of Christ-loving saints as the very bait that leads them into a state of bondage.

> In the end, though we apply effort, discipline, and training, it is still God's Grace freely extended unto which produces the fruit.

## A Working Mission Statement

When I was in my early twenties, I was captivated by a book written by Simon Sinek titled, *Start with Why*. The premise is that we must understand deeply why we are doing something if we are to have any hope for remaining focused or to possess the grit required to endure until we have reached our destination. Simon writes, "All organizations start with WHY, but only the great ones keep their WHY clear year after year. Those who forget WHY they were founded show up to the race every day to outdo someone else instead of to outdo themselves. The pursuit, for those who lose sight of WHY they are running the race, is for the medal or to beat someone else." It goes without saying that we are not an organization, but the principles still apply. First, if you forget why you've chosen to be a disciple and follow Jesus' way of living, there will be plenty of reasons to stop and begin following an easier or seemingly more lucrative way of living. Secondly, if you make discipleship about anything or anyone other than yourself, and who you are becoming in Christ, you will fall quickly into legalism, bitterness, and frustration. Discipleship, as we'll see, is first and foremost about *you*.

Before attempting to explore the tangibles, we need to have our 'why' established. Maybe you'd like to press pause and think about this for yourself for a while, or perhaps it's something that you should seek in prayer. This needs to be deeply personal and convicting for you. I'll share with you my 'why' and we will use it as an outline to explore and establish the tangibles moving forward. The reason why I choose to be a disciple serves also as an outline of how I go about being a disciple. I am a disciple **"to become like Jesus internally by being with Jesus eternally so that I might live like Jesus externally."**

**Have a Plan**

First and foremost, we must have for ourselves a strategically established plan designed for the purpose of becoming like Jesus. One does not simply get saved on

## A Vision for Becoming

Sunday and wake up on Monday with a completely new set of desires, values, habits, disciplines, attitudes, behaviors, and intentions any more than a young physician becomes a proficient and competent surgeon the day after medical school. When we read the gospels and see Jesus' modeling for us who we can also be with maturity—such as one who overcomes temptations, takes authority over demons and disease, remains gentle and kind in the midst of stress, forgives his murderers, sleeps in storms, loves those who use and abuse him, and so on—we are in essence seeing Jesus on game day. Let me explain what I mean by that.

Growing up, I was an avid soccer player. I loved that sport, and from what others told me, there was a time when I had quite the potential. I remember watching iconic players such as Pele, Landon Donovan, Messi, and Ronaldo, fantasizing about being the next player to take the league by storm. My path, however, would not lead me to that end. Why? Primarily because the path to becoming the next Messi was not found in simply performing on game day. The path was found in doing what Messi did off the field and outside of game day which enabled him to be who he was on game day. I was not equipped nor prepared to train like Messi when no one was watching; therefore, I could never hope to execute like Messi when everyone was watching. In much the same way, the character and accomplishments of Christ that we read in the gospels come from His way of living, that is, His training

> I was not equipped nor prepared to train like Messi when no one was watching.

and disciplines, that are subtly and much less often highlighted throughout the same pages. In short, we cannot expect to be like Christ on game day (i.e., moments of testing, adversity, or pressure) if we are not prepared to train like Christ in the off-season.

Therefore, if we possess within our hearts a vision to be like Christ as we see Him displayed in the gospels—that is, loving, gentle, kind, generous, disciplined, and walking in authority—then we must have a plan that leads us to that end. After all, "A goal without a plan is just a wish." - Antoine de Saint-Exupéry. So, what's your plan to become like Jesus? How are you measuring your growth? Again, pastors, what is your plan to make mature light-producing, fruit-bearing followers of the way of Jesus out of those in your congregation? Though there is value in our weekend gatherings and classroom setting attempts, the truth is it will require more than that to effectively teach and show our congregants the way of living in Christ. Discipleship is not taking a spiritual gifts test to identify where someone might fit best in serving your organization. Perhaps it will include that—serving the local body can be quite a powerful discipline—but I'm afraid too many pastors have made discipleship about filling heads with knowledge rather than hearts with virtue. Too many pastors have been content to measure discipleship by how much someone is involved or 'plugged-in' to their church all the while divorce rates soar, greed thrives, hostile attitudes prevail, suicide rates climb, depression and anxiety dominate, and lust rules over the lives of the same congregants who they thought were "on fire for Jesus" and shockingly, pastors are left baffled by this. The sad truth is we largely have not prioritized our

## Becoming Like Jesus Internally

The goal, the *raison d'être* of discipleship is to become like Jesus internally. We must understand this. If we fall into the terrible trap that living like Jesus externally is the goal, we will go about living as a disciple all wrong. We will slip into trying and forget all about training. It is through trying to live like Jesus without prioritizing becoming like Him that we end up in legalism, bondage, burnout, and shame. Jesus teaches that it is not the act that defiles, for the act is merely the proof that someone is defiled. *"Nothing that enters a man from the outside can defile him; but the things that come out of a man, these are what defile him."* (Mark 7:15) The entire point of Jesus' famous Sermon on the Mount in Matthew 5-7 was that inward transformation must be accomplished before outward transformation could be realized. Our hearts and minds must be renewed first, for only by it will our lives experience transformation. (cf. Romans 12:2).

The work of inner transformation must be accomplished by the Spirit. The inner immaterial world of the human soul is a complex phenomenon that can never be fully known or understood. The scary truth is that we are capable of knowing very little about the condition or qualities of our own soul, much less someone else's (another reason not to cast judgements). How then, if our spirit is unsearchable, do we ever stand a chance at inner transformation? It is precisely here that we come to understand the profound impact of the prayer of the Psalmist which implores the Spirit to *"search me and know me, see if there be any wicked way in me."* (cf. Psalm 139:23-24)

Dr. Willard describes the renovated and inhabited heart as the "only real hope of humanity on earth." This is because it is precisely by the renovation of our hearts that we are transformed, and it is in the transformed heart that the Son, together with the Father and the Spirit, dwells with a mighty influence and power that can then be converted from the immaterial universe into the material. Peter teaches that when we are "known" (an idiom for sexual intimacy in which a seed is deposited into the womb) by God, we are then born again, not of the human seed which perishes, but of an imperishable seed that is conceived in the womb of the heart. By this spiritual process, we are born again not of flesh and blood, but of the Spirit, and it is precisely this process that Jesus teaches Nicodemus must occur for one to enter the Kingdom of the Heavens (see John 3). It is in this way that we are made "new creations" as Paul teaches (2 Corinthians 5:17). We are new creations not in the body primarily but in the spirit, and from this immaterial transformation, the material world has a newfound hope of encountering God through His imagers. So then, how can we become like Jesus? In short, we can't.

**Being with Jesus Eternally**

The goal of discipleship is to become like Jesus internally, but the prize of discipleship is being with Jesus eternally.

## A Vision for Becoming

Not only is it the prize, but it is the very means by which we are transformed. Our transformation, remember, is accomplished by Him, through His Spirit, according to His Grace, but this does not mean that we don't play a role in the process. We in fact play a critical role in the process; it's just not the part that actually does the transforming. We are only required to *do* two things. First, we must seek, and second, we must obey.

The psalmist gives us the secret, *"Delight yourself in the LORD, and He will give you the desires of your heart."* (Psalm 37:4) When we seek the Lord and make Him our delight, He then comes in and changes the very fabric of our DNA. Our desires at their root begin to transform into His desires for us, and from here we become people who should be able to always "do whatever we want." The scriptures are littered with teachings on the importance of seeking God and its direct link to inner transformation; for example, Hosea proclaimed:

> *Sow righteousness for yourselves, reap the fruit of unfailing love, and break up your unplowed ground; for it is time to seek the Lord until he comes and showers his righteousness on you.* (Hosea 10:12)

In John chapter 15, Jesus teaches that we must *"abide in Him"* if we wish to produce fruit (external living).

What is seeking and how do we do it? In some sense, seeking and training are synonymous. At its core, seeking God is the engagement in a thing that only we can do which positions us in such a way that God's Spirit can now do in us what only He can do. In this, we find the value of those activities which are often referred to as "spiritual disciplines". Prayer, fasting, communion, solitude, silence, generosity, and the practice of virtue (see 1 Corinthians 13, Galatians 5:22, and Colossians 3:12-15 to start) are all ways in which we may train and seek. They in and of themselves do not merit us favor or earn us a higher standing in God's sight. These activities are merely our way of doing what we can so He can do in us what we can't.

**Living Like Jesus Externally**

If the goal of discipleship is to become like Jesus internally, and the means of inner transformation is being with Jesus, then the effect of discipleship is living like Jesus externally.

Seeking, as previously discussed, leads to inner transformation, and our inner transformation leads to our ability to obey. As we seek, He will speak. In the process of maturation and transformation, the Lord will give us direction and responsibilities, and when He does, we must be prepared to obey. Obedience is where we grow the most and the fastest. All of Jesus' "game-day" moments in the gospels, those awe-inspiring examples of how we desire to live, are moments in which Jesus is obeying the Father. Jesus says, *"I love the Father and do exactly what my Father has commanded me."* (John 14:31), and again He says:

> *So Jesus replied, "Truly, truly, I tell you, the Son can do nothing by Himself unless He sees the Father doing it. For whatever the Father does, the Son also does."* (John 5:19)

Obedience is the game-day moment we prepare for, so when it comes, lean in and know that your obedience will bless lives and glorify the Father.

## A Vision for Becoming

The purpose of fruit production and light-bearing, which is in essence our faith working through love, is singular. It is for the glory of the Father through the edifying of His creation. We have the honor of engaging in the Father's glorification in a myriad of ways, but to summarize, we serve others from a place of compassion, and secondly, we become a model for younger disciples to imitate.

Jesus placed a high emphasis on serving. The night before His death, Jesus washed the disciples' feet and delivered his final lesson:

> *You call Me Teacher and Lord, and rightly so, because I am. So, if I, your Lord and Teacher, have washed your feet, you also should wash one another's feet. I have set you an example so that you should do as I have done for you.* (John 13:13-15)

Though we are called to serve, we must follow Jesus in our service to others, and Jesus always served from a place of compassion. The authors of the synoptic gospels tell us numerous times that Jesus performed His miracles from a place of deep compassion. For instance, Matthew shares with his readers, *"When He saw the crowds, He was moved with compassion for them, because they were harassed and helpless, like sheep without a shepherd."* (Matthew 9:36)

Finally, the great commission is clear. We must go make disciples as we ourselves grow as a disciple. What is the primary means we do this? Through setting an example for others to imitate. Sure, teaching can be useful and in some sense knowledge and theory are fundamental, but as we've mentioned before, humans are designed to imitate. Therefore, I invite you to step into the role of a mentor and teacher to whomever God has placed in your sphere of influence, be it a child, a co-worker, an in-law, or a friend. Allow the light that God's Spirit is producing in you to be set upon a hill and seen for God to be glorified and to serve as an example for others to imitate.

"I'd rather see a sermon than hear one any day. I'd rather one would walk with me than merely tell me the way." - Edgar Guest

**The Key to Endurance and Growth**

"There is immense power when a group of people with similar interests gets together to work toward the same goals." - Idowu Koyenikan

> Love, real self-sacrificing love, is a very difficult discipline to master.

In conclusion, how can we realistically expect to endure walking as a disciple? Perhaps one of the hardest things one will ever do is continue in their discipleship to Christ because it requires maturing in one's ability to love. Love, real self-sacrificing love, is a very difficult discipline to master; especially when the object of your love is your enemy. Yet, Jesus gave us this example by dying for us on the cross while we were yet His enemies, so that standard is set.

We ought not to fret, however, for in His wisdom God established a solution to our inevitable weariness in doing good. His solution is community. That's right, the gathering of the saints. Although the gathering during the first few hundred years of the church was much different than the one we recognize today. Not to suggest our manner of gathering today is wrong or inferior, I happen to believe, in fact, quite the opposite. Rather, I merely mean to point out that the gathering in the first century was specifically designed in such a way that it provided a trellis of sorts to the believer which would enable them to have the support they needed to endure in love and good deeds.

Notice that for the author of Hebrews, which most believe to be the apostle Paul, the premier purpose of the gathering was not to worship or preach sermons. Now, of course, those things are central and ought to be done, especially in the context of community; however, in the letter we gain insight into the fact that the gathering was to serve as our means for endurance in a particular way of living as Christ's disciple:

> *And let us consider how to <u>spur one another on to love and good deeds</u>. Let us not neglect meeting together, as some have made a habit, but let us encourage one another, and all the more as you see the Day approaching.* (Hebrews 10:24-25)

For this biblical author, the power of the gathering was in its ability to provide a place to encourage one another and to *spur one another* on to love and good deeds. In the first century, there was an emphasis placed on meeting in homes. This might not have been intentional as much as it was due to practicalities. In most cases, it was because Christians were being persecuted so they were forced underground, or venues for large gatherings were scarce or unavailable. However, if the early church had a choice to meet in a large amphitheater once per week or at homes dispersed throughout the city every day of the week, I believe they would have chosen the latter 100% of the time.

## *The* INVITATION

We are given a beautiful picture in Acts 2 of the church blossoming in its communal context:

> *All the believers were together and had everything in common. Selling their possessions and goods, they shared with anyone who was in need. With one accord they continued to meet daily in the temple courts and to break bread from house to house, sharing their meals with gladness and sincerity of heart praising God, and enjoying the favor of all the people. And the Lord added to their number daily those who were being saved.* (Acts 2:43-47)

In the context of community, needs are much easier to meet because they become much easier to identify. Furthermore, in a community, one is much more easily challenged or provoked to love and good deeds. This is because in the context of community, people have access to your context and your world. They know where you're being challenged and stressed. Additionally, they are more likely to know when someone has treated you wrongly, and they are much more readily able to encourage you to respond in love rather than in vengeance.

Finally, when people who carry the same ambition gather, no matter how few, they become very powerful in their ability to effect change and make an impact. Idowu Koyenikan once wrote, "A community that is engaged and working together can be a powerful force." This is precisely why no one among the earliest group of believers had any need and, furthermore, it is why the number of Christians was growing rapidly each day. Therefore, we need a community in which we can confess our shortcomings and our needs. We need a space in which

## A Vision for Becoming

we can hear of and meet the needs of others. This space should be a place where people can easily gain knowledge of our trials and victories, as well as our temptations and failures. It should be a place where others can see if our life is progressively producing fruit or growing stagnant. A community should be a place where we are encouraged and spurred onward in our maturation process as light-producing disciples of Christ.

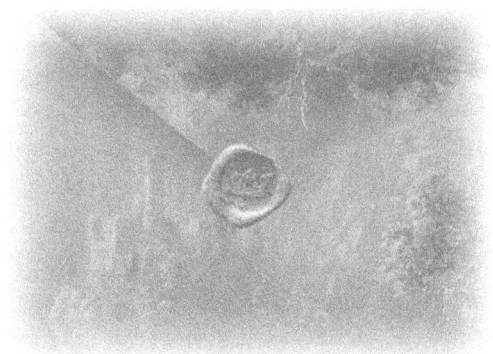

# 9. Why A Disciple?

> *The greatest issue facing the world today, with all its heartbreaking needs, is whether those who, by profession or culture, are identified as 'Christians' will become disciples – students, apprentices, practitioners – of Jesus Christ, steadily learning from him how to live the life of the Kingdom of the Heavens into every corner of human existence.-*
> Dallas Willard, *The Great Omission*

I'd like to say at the outset of this chapter that much of what I have learned surrounding this topic of discipleship comes from a man whom I've quoted several times already and will likely continue to do so for the next chapter or two. Dallas Willard has more to say about discipleship, the kingdom of God, and true transformation than I could ever hope to say, and he articulates it much better too. I am greatly indebted to him. I would like to point you to his book *The Great Omission* for further study on this topic.

## *The* INVITATION

The reason I am writing this book is because I have a conviction that many Christians do not know or live in their identity. The two categories that address our identity in Christ as a citizen and an inheritance are largely not taught in mainstream Christianity. It's, of course, a terrible thing that any aspect of our identity is left untaught, but perhaps something far worse is that the concepts of our identity as children and disciples are talked about quite often, even to the point of being labeled as 'ultra-trendy' topics in the church. Yet, these two topics are often left impractical and ambiguous, as if we are being taught in metaphors or symbolic language. In some circles, they are even becoming known as "clichés." Worse yet, many in the church today would quickly identify themselves as a disciple or a child, yet they have very little idea how to articulate what that means and even less of an idea as to their plan for practically living out their life as an intentional child or disciple.

A core reason for my belief that we have many Christians but few disciples of Christ is because of the growing chasm in our world today between the expressed theology and doctrine of professing believers and the expressed character and nature of professing believers. No doubt you've experienced this in your lifetime. It causes a great deal of frustration and pain when a 'Christian' acts like a pagan, doesn't it? Especially when doing so towards another supposed 'brother' or 'sister' in Christ? Why does this problem exist and continue to increase? I'd wager that it is simply because we are not being taught or shown how to follow Jesus in practical everyday living. We have no 'fathers,' as Paul calls them, to imitate. Human beings are designed to imitate. We were created with these things called mirror neurons which, in oversimplified terms, wire us by instinct to imitate that which we see, especially as young babes. Throughout scripture, 'child' is used as a metaphor to describe one who imitates, and a 'father' describes the one who is watched and imitated. This is why Paul tells those he is discipling to "imitate me and I imitate Christ." The idea was that those imitating him would one day be the type of person whom others could imitate, much like Timothy. However, we cannot be too upset with the previous generation of Christians, because they, of course, had the same problem when they were young in their faith. How then do we solve this cyclical problem? The answer is a system called discipleship.

Can you imagine going your entire life genuinely believing you were a disciple of Christ but one day, towards the end, realizing that you were indeed a disciple, but not to Jesus? I am reminded of the Ice Age movie in which Ellie, a female mammoth who is raised by opossums, genuinely believes she is an opossum until one day she recognizes, through examining her footprint, that she is not. Similarly, many God-fearing, Jesus-loving, and well-meaning Christians identify themselves as disciples of Christ, but in fact, they are not. Identity is not measured by self-identification but in how one lives and the features one possesses which stem from the fabric of their nature. For instance, I can identify as a dog, but

> Identity is not measured by self-identification but in how one lives and the features one possesses which stem from the fabric of their nature.

that does not make me a dog. I may identify as a dog for lovely reasons such as, I genuinely love dogs and desire their good, yet this is not enough to make me a dog. A dog has a unique set of features, behaviors, and characteristics that make them distinct; and so then does a disciple of Christ.

**The Divorce from Discipleship**

We are all disciples of something; the question is, "What are we a disciple of?" I mentioned earlier how it would be devastating to go one's entire life thinking they were a disciple of Christ just to find out towards the end that they were indeed a disciple but not of Christ. For many Christians, their discipleship to Christ begins and ends at the label with which they proudly associate themselves. To say, "I am a disciple of Jesus" for most merely means "I am a Christian and I do my best to do Christian things." In fact, the terms Christian and disciple ought to be synonymous since the term Christian was created specifically to label and identify those who followed Christ. Today, however, one can be a Christian without being much of a disciple of Christ at all. We have made this possible in our modern day, but it was never so in the first century and through the first several hundred years of the church. It most certainly was not a concept the Biblical authors had in mind. No, for the apostles, one was only labeled as a Christian, by outsiders mind you, because they could be clearly recognized as a disciple of Christ.

Our great divorce from discipleship largely comes from a teaching that says one must merely agree to a particular set of information (i.e., believe) and you're set for all eternity. Therefore, the natural rebuttal to discipleship was born: "If all I need to do for salvation is believe, then discipleship is not necessary." Firstly, to believe in a biblical sense is not to affirm a set of facts as being true. To believe is to rely upon and to live in accordance with one's reliance. For instance, if my home has two levels and I am downstairs enjoying a cup of tea when, all of a sudden, a booming voice comes ringing from up the staircase proclaiming the good news of "Lee, the CEO of Porsche is driving around the neighborhood and whoever comes out to greet him will get a free car of their choosing!" I will either rely upon that word (i.e., testimony) or I can reject that word; either way, my actions will naturally follow the choice I have made in my heart. Reliance upon Christ works in a similar fashion. **If you believe His words, you will do His words.**

Secondly, this idea comes from a failure to recognize that discipleship is a gift of love that we offer unto Christ and the Father, not something we do as a sort of 'price to pay' in exchange for eternal life. Those operating under the ideology of "discipleship is unnecessary" tread dangerous waters because, as Dallas Willard says, we become a sort of "vampire Christian" who in essence says, "I will take a little of your blood Lord, and I'll see you in the next life." This, of course, is not the intent of most Christians, yet unknowingly we - when we are not intentional about our identity as disciples – live according to this attitude.

**What is Discipleship?**

Let me now begin discussing what a disciple is with two quotes by, you guessed it, Dallas Willard. First, "Disciples of Jesus are people who do not just profess certain views as their own but apply their growing understanding of life in the Kingdom of the Heavens to every aspect of their life on earth." And second, "The disciple is one who, intent upon becoming Christ-like and so dwelling in his 'faith and practice', systematically and progressively rearranges his affairs to that end."

So we begin with the questions: do we actually desire to be like Christ, and how do we intend to progress towards this end?

Jesus' great commission to his followers, that is, His final command, was to *"Go and make disciples."* He was not interested in converts, but disciples. How, though, was one to be a disciple or lead another into discipleship to Christ? *"...baptizing them in the name of the Father, Son, and the Holy Spirit"* and *"...teaching them to do all that I have commanded."* (Matthew 28:19-20) Jesus gives two practical steps to discipleship here. First, baptizing, which I won't discuss at length here other than to say this isn't mostly referring to dipping someone in water. The command here is not to baptize in water but into the 'name.' This has a more profound meaning and, quite honestly, a meaning that makes much more sense in the context of His mission than the idea of submerging someone in water. However, I'm much more interested in the second command.

Jesus was a rabbi, which means 'teacher'; yes, but think of a rabbi as more of an expert who, after mastering a concept or way of life, would gather a small group of students with the goal of passing along the things in which they had become proficient. That small group of students was known in Hebrew as 'talmidim,' which means disciples. A rabbi had one primary goal for their disciples, and that was, in essence, to create clones who would re-present their rabbi after he had passed away. The rabbi wanted their disciples not just to know what they knew, but to first think the way they thought and then to embody their very character and eventually create more disciples who follow the way of the original rabbi. Jesus, as a rabbi, wants much of the same things for his disciples. He wants His disciples to 'abide in Him' and to allow His words to 'remain in them' after He had ascended to heaven so that they might be the continuation of the incarnation in the earth, producing fruit and light unto the glory of the Father.

A disciple, therefore, is an apprentice. An apprentice is not someone interested in learning theory but is rather someone interested in learning a way of thinking which results in the ability to live and conduct certain tasks skillfully. An apprentice is more than a student, for a student gathers knowledge, while an apprentice, at least in ancient times, would not simply show up for class and go home. They would oftentimes live with their rabbi and observe them day and night, in good times and bad, under stress or in times of great joy, for the purpose of one day imitating them. Jesus says, *"A disciple is not above his teacher, but everyone who is fully trained will <u>be like</u> his teacher."* (Luke 6:40) Discipleship is the process of intentional and progressive training to be like one's teacher. It is not to know what the teacher knows but to be like the teacher, and from becoming like the teacher (internally), one then lives like the teacher (externally).

One might also define discipleship as "the part we play in the sequential process of sanctification, which is the putting off of the human nature and the putting on of the holy nature that was made available to us through Christ and the ever-present Kingdom of Heaven."

**What Does a Disciple Look Like?**

Someone who walks in their identity as a disciple can be easily distinguished from the modern-day Christian. This is the very reason the term Christian was created, to begin with. It was a term that was used to denote and, in most cases, mock one who was a follower of what the book of Acts calls "The Way." Followers of "The Way" were those who followed Christ into His way of living from the Kingdom of Heaven towards the earth. For this reason, Paul urges his students in Corinth by saying:

> *That is why I have sent you Timothy, my beloved and faithful child in the Lord. He will remind you of <u>my way of life in Christ Jesus</u>, which is exactly what I teach everywhere in every church.* (1 Corinthians 4:17)

Notice that Paul doesn't teach a doctrine to memorize or a theology to "believe." He primarily teaches <u>a way of living in Christ Jesus</u>. A disciple is known by their way of living, much like a gentile identified a Jew by their distinct way of living.

## Why A Disciple?

What, then, is this way of living? There are two layers to this answer. First, the way of living refers to how a disciple trains, and second, the "way of living" refers to who you become as a result of your training. We will explore some ways to train in the succeeding chapter, but for now, I'd like to focus on the end result of discipleship. Paul spends a great deal of time teaching the type of person we ought to be by teaching how we should live. For instance,

> *Do nothing out of selfish ambition or empty pride, but in humility consider others more important than yourselves. Each of you should look not only to your own interests, but also to the interests of others.* (Philippians 2:3-4)

*"Do everything without complaining or arguing."* (Philippians 2:14) – When was the last time you met someone who was as serious about being this type of person as someone on a new diet or workout routine?

> *Therefore, as the elect of God, holy and beloved, clothe yourselves with hearts of compassion, kindness, humility, gentleness, and patience. Bear with one another and forgive any complaint you may have against someone else. Forgive as the Lord forgave you. And over all these virtues put on love, which is the bond of perfect unity. Let the peace of Christ rule in your hearts, for to this you were called as members of one body. And be thankful.* (Colossians 3:12-15)

The list could go on and on, but lest I quote nearly the entirety of Paul's letters, I will stop there. The first step to truly walking in our identity as disciples is to stop viewing the Bible as a list of commands or do's and don'ts,

> The goal of the gospel is to transform people with human tendencies into a new creation...

and to begin seeing it as a mirror reflecting the type of person you were made to become through the work of Christ, His Spirit, and the Grace of God. He's not looking for people with human tendencies to *try* and do these things. The goal of the gospel is to transform people with human tendencies into a new creation, that is, those who have new, holy tendencies.

Therefore, the primary way we distinguish a disciple from someone who wears only the name is by their way of living, that is, their fruit. Jesus teaches this multiple times throughout His earthly ministry. In Matthew He says, *"Beware of false prophets. They come to you in sheep's clothing, but inwardly they are ravenous wolves. By their fruit you will recognize them."* (Matthew 7:15) And again, in John He teaches, *"This is to My Father's glory, that you bear much fruit, proving yourselves to be My disciples."* (John 15:8) Fruit, yes, is a way of living, but it is specifically a way of living that is produced from love. This is why Jesus simultaneously teaches that *"By this everyone will know that you are My disciples, if you love one another."* (John 13:35)

In essence, the deep craving and the intense yearning of a disciple is to put Jesus' teaching into practice. Upon concluding His famous Sermon on the Mount Jesus says:

> *Therefore, everyone who hears these words of Mine and acts on them is like a wise man who built his house on the rock. The rain fell, the torrents raged,*

## Why A Disciple?

*and the winds blew and beat against that house; yet it did not fall, because its foundation was on the rock.*

*But everyone who hears these words of Mine and does not act on them is like a foolish man who built his house on sand. The rain fell, the torrents raged, and the winds blew and beat against that house, and it fell—and great was its collapse!* (Matthew 7:24-27)

A disciple is one who recognizes Jesus as their rabbi and thus desires to live the life He lived, so they intentionally plan to practice His way of living in the expectation of experiencing the abundant life He provided. A great litmus test offered by Dr. Willard for whether we are walking in our identity as a disciple goes as such: "Examination of our ultimate *desires*, and *intentions*, reflected in the specific *responses* and *choices* that make up our lives, can show whether there are things we hold more important than being like Him."

As we draw to the conclusion of this chapter, I must present a warning. Though someone indeed walking in their identity as a disciple will produce fruit, that does not mean they will be fully mature in their sanctification process. We must do well to remember that we are all on a progressive journey in our maturation; therefore, a true disciple is first identified in the hidden recesses of the motives and intentions of the heart. Though they may not act as a disciple in one moment does not mean we have sufficient evidence of a "Christian in name only." Perhaps the same individual who failed to act like their rabbi genuinely desires and intends to mature and live like their rabbi. This intention is pure, but it is unseen because it exists in the heart. God alone sees the heart; therefore, we mustn't allow fruit (the visible evidence of the invisible transformed heart) to be a means by which we judge another. Let's move on now to discussing in a more practical way how we might live out our identity as a child.

# Category Four: Children

# 10. Child: What is My Father Like?

"A child of the King shouldn't live like a slave of the world." – Unknown

One of the few things every human on earth can share as a common experience is that of being a child. The experiences we had as children, however, have a wide range. As we approach this category, I must implore you to lay aside your experiences as a child and not allow yourself to project them onto your identity as a child of God. Further, and perhaps more importantly, you must find within yourself the ability to put aside your memories and experiences of your earthly father, as they, whether good or bad, must not be projected onto our understanding of God as our Father. It is crucial that we see God and His role as our Father accurately if we are to understand the depths of our identity as children in God's family, and unfortunately, our earthly father does not present an accurate representation of our heavenly father. A common issue I come across in the counseling clinic, for those who are Christian, is that in many cases, those who have areas of major pain or bondage in their life, also have associated with those same areas, an idea about God that they deem to be true stemming from what was true of their earthly father. In other words, because they believed God their Father must be like the only other experience they have had with a father, they cannot experience freedom until they think rightly about God. They are imprisoned by their belief of not who God is but what God is like.

Those who fall victim to this trap, which is likely most of us at some point in time, find themselves in the same predicament as the poor steward in Jesus' parable. In Matthew 25, we're told a parable of multiple servants who were given a satchel of talents, each with a different amount. Each servant was given a chance to steward the money until their master returned. The one who had received the least buried his talents, which of course we then find out was a bad choice. Why, though, did he bury them? The parable tells us:

> *Finally, the servant who had received the one talent came and said, "Master, I knew that you are a <u>hard man</u>, reaping where you have not sown and gathering where you have not scattered seed."* (Matthew 25:24)

The servant's choice to bury the talents was influenced by his idea of what kind of person the master was. For this reason, it is critical not just that we understand what God is (i.e., father, king, etc.) but also who God is and, by that, I mean what kind of personality, character, and nature He possesses. In other words, "what is God like?"

### Child: What is My Father Like?

Much of a child's identity is determined by the identity of their father (and mother, of course). Therefore, to clearly grasp our own identity, we must briefly discuss the identity of our Father and its implications upon us. Let me first add, however, that each of the elements we are about to discuss can be said of the mother as well; therefore, note that my sole focus on a father here is not an attempt to minimize the role of a mother but to teach about our Father in Heaven.

**How a Father Shapes a Child's Identity**

There are at least five key areas in which a father directly impacts the identity of their children.

**First**, the father affects cultural influence and social status. A father's reputation, profession, wealth, and status all have effects on his children. A child will inherit a status or a title in the eyes of society that is much in line with their father's. Additionally, a child inherits cultural attributes such as values, customs, behaviors, priorities, and celebrations.

**Second**, the father greatly shapes emotional and psychological factors. A father is a role model from whom the children learn what kind of person they ought to be, and additionally for girls, what kind of man they ought to marry. They learn right from wrong, and they learn how to see the world around them through taking on the worldview of their father. If the father is a naturally trusting person, the child may see other humans as inherently good with some exceptions, while a father who is not a trusting person may influence their child to view humanity as inherently bad with some good exceptions. How, then, does our Father in Heaven see other humans, and have we learned to share His perspective? Furthermore, a father's strengths, weaknesses, and character traits are often absorbed and replicated by the child. This dynamic process of replication is designed by God Himself as a fundamental aspect of God's kingdom expansion process, which occurs via childbearing.

> Nearly all of those I work with as a counselor have some form of presenting issue that stems from how they were psychologically shaped by their father or the lack thereof.

From a psychological dimension, a father's presence or absence and the quality of the father-child relationship have profound effects on the child's self-esteem, self-confidence, mental health and stability, emotional security, and overall sense of value. Without exaggeration, nearly all of those I work with as a counselor have some form of presenting issue that stems from how they were psychologically shaped by their father or the lack thereof. The father's effect on one's psychological formation is so great that we now have entire philosophical approaches to psychotherapy centered on exploring, in depth, the world of the inner child and its experiences during the young and impressionable years as a means for correcting the adverse symptoms experienced in adulthood.

It is no secret that a child who feels accepted and valued by their father is more likely to develop a positive self-identity, which has a host of beneficial by-products. For instance, someone with a positive self-identity is more likely to take the risks in life that are necessary for productivity and satisfaction. Something as commonplace as getting married or having a child, either through natural means or adoption, is loaded with risk, yet we move in those directions to reap the fulfilling joy that comes with them. That is, however, unless one does not possess a positive self-identity.

In the event someone is found to be lacking, they will follow patterns of isolation, hoarding, and paralysis so far as it relates to life changes and lack of trust, even of close loved ones. As a result, these people often go through life unfulfilled and unsatisfied, which leads to behaviors of self-gratification. Dallas Willard once wrote, "…failure to attain a deeply satisfying life always has the effect of making sinful actions seem good." He continues later to conclude that, "…our success in overcoming temptation will be easier if we are basically happy in our lives." Thus, we can see how every sin is indeed a choice we make to fulfill a desire or unmet need. Indeed, the apostle James knew what he was talking about when he wrote.

> *But each one is tempted when by his own evil desires, he is lured away and enticed. Then after desire has conceived, it gives birth to sin; and sin, when it is full-grown, gives birth to death.* (James 1:14-15)

**Third**, the father heavily influences their child's spiritual identity. In saying this, I do not only mean religious identity, though that is certainly true, but more importantly, I intend to highlight the effect a father has on the spirit of a person. The spirit can be likened to the executive or command center of the person. It is the place in which the will and intentions are created, housed, and impressed upon the other bodily faculties. Scripture will often interchange the term spirit with the term heart to denote the centrality of the spirit to the human make-up.

It is my conviction that the spirit is the highest aspect of the human essence and life; therefore, its effects on the body, mind, and emotions will be immense. I'm not the only one who thinks this, however. Secular psychology also affirms similar notions. Abraham Maslow, an influential American psychologist, is credited for saying:

> The so-called spiritual or "higher" life is on the same continuum with the life of the flesh, the "lower life." The spiritual life is part of the biological life. It is the "highest" part of it… The spiritual life is of the human essence. It is a defining characteristic of the human nature without which the human nature is not full human nature. It is part of the real self, of one's identity, of one's inner core, one's species hood, of full humanness."[3]

Since the spirit is thought of as the "higher" life, it makes sense that the condition of the spirit would have effects on every other aspect of the human essence. Many come to receive counseling, and they are surprised to learn that what brought them to counseling was not the actual issue in need of attention.

I was once working with a gentleman who expressed that his increasing anger was what led him to seek counseling. After a few sessions working with him, we discovered that it was not his anger in need of therapy but rather his anger was simply the spirit's way of manifesting in

---

[3] Abraham Maslow, "The Good Life of the Self-Actualizing Person", The Humanist (July-August, 1967): 139.

the material what was true of its condition in the realm that the spirit resides. Come to find out, the gentleman had trouble with control and being controlled. This, of course, was being inflamed due to a medical condition that he couldn't control nor find a solution for. What we learned together is that his spirit hadn't learned to be content in adverse or uncomfortable circumstances, nor had he learned to surrender uncontrollable circumstances to a higher authority that he could rely on, namely Christ. Therefore, the condition of the spirit made itself known through anger and other attempts to control his circumstances. When the spirit was taken into consideration and offered value and support, the other human faculties (i.e., mind and emotions) were also positively impacted.

I say all of this to support the notion that the spirit is perhaps the most important faculty of the human, and how it is shaped and taken care of will have implications on the rest of our human essence and experience. Therefore, the father's role in influencing the spirit of a child is of utmost importance. I hope that by now you are beginning to see that for each of these categories, there is a parallel between the impact of an earthly father on their child and the impact of our heavenly Father on His children.

**Fourth**, the father has an economic effect on their children. The impact that money has on one's life experience is substantial. The resources a father has at his disposal directly affect their child's world. As a result of wealth, a child may be placed in a more favorable position for success, productivity, and advancement due to the education, resources, and people the child of a wealthy father may have access to. Conversely, a child whose father lacks resources and opportunity may have a more difficult time succeeding in life. A father who lacks wealth has benefits, however; that is because economic wealth is not the only nor the greatest form of wealth. A father lacking monetary assets is still able to deposit into their child principles and ethics that may lead them to much success. Children from both backgrounds must learn how to work hard, be honest and humble, and develop resilience and responsibility if they hope to live a prosperous life for any length of time.

**Fifth**, the father will play a role in how the child is perceived by others in a social context. Much like in our first category, a child will inherit an image or a reputation in the eyes of society that is akin to how society views their father, that is, at least until they can establish their own identity within society later in life. The reputation one has is denoted by how someone else *feels* when they think about you. The core concept we must come away with here is that society will relate to you based on how it relates to your father. As children of God, this plays out negatively more than positively so long as we reside on the fallen earth. Jesus warns those who are to become children of His Father:

> *If the world hates you, you know that it has hated Me before you. If you were of the world, it would love you as its own. Instead, the world hates you, because you are not of the world, but I have chosen you out of the world.* (John 15:18-19)

His word of wisdom was, in essence, this: "My Father, and I as His son, are hated from a societal standpoint. If you wish to become children of my Father, you too will share His reputation in the eyes of society." The prophet Isaiah foretold of Jesus' unfavorable social status: *"He was despised and rejected by men... Like one from whom men hide their faces, He was despised, and we esteemed Him not."* (Isaiah 53:3-4) It is when society begins to see God for who He truly is through children who accurately bear His image that society will develop a new reputation of Him. However, there are forces in direct opposition to our Father that we will never escape, that is, of course, until they finally meet their fate.

**Our Father, A King**

So then, we must now discuss briefly who our Father is and, with the previous factors in mind, what effect it has on His children. As we discussed in chapter two, the entire story of the Bible is focused on a kingdom. God, our Father, above all else in the narrative of scripture, is a king. This is, of course, exciting news since in the same way there are influences a father's identity has on their child's identity, there are involuntary effects on the child when your father is a king. There are several areas in which the identity of a king's child is shaped, as well as their experiences, due to their father's identity.

**First**, they inherit a royal status and privilege. From the time of birth, royal children are groomed and trained for leadership. They have much to learn about the kingdom, its people, traditions, values, law, culture, and so forth. They will one day be responsible for not just maintaining the kingdom but also advancing the kingdom. These same things must occur when one is born again into the Kingdom of Heaven. We are not born again into a status of maturity in which we are instantly ready for leadership and to carry authority in the same way a natural infant isn't ready for such responsibility. However, we as royal children have access now to the greatest of instructors.

**Second**, they are heirs and successors, and as such, they are viewed from a young age as a future king or queen. They also see themselves as a king or queen long before they assume the position legally. Because of this, they begin to act as though they were king or queen at young ages, holding themselves to higher standards both in conduct and character. For instance, a normal citizen may eat something that has quickly fallen on the floor, especially if they didn't know when they'd get their next meal. However, a child of a king would never stoop so low; they'd simply eat a fresh form of food from their surplus. They adjust their way of living according to how they view themselves.

**Third**, they are, from birth, public figures who serve as images of their kingdom's culture, values, and priorities. As royalty, the child is not just a private individual but a public figure who often becomes a symbol of the nation itself. Their identity is intertwined with the cultural, religious, and historical symbolism of the monarchy, and their actions are scrutinized as reflections of national values.

**Fourth**, children of kings receive a royal education and training. Children of kings usually receive an education tailored not just to academic excellence but to prepare them for leadership. This education shapes their intellectual identity, making them knowledgeable in areas like statecraft, diplomacy, and military strategy. Often, royal children are also trained in moral and ethical codes tied to their role as future rulers, shaping their values and character.

**Fifth**, the child is instantly connected to the historical legacy of their family and responsible for the part they will play in the continuation of the legacy. This comes with implications. The child of the king is expected to carry forth the reputation of those who came before them. They are expected to uphold and enhance their family's honor by representing them well. In the same manner, we represent our Father and His kingdom as foreigners on the earth. The great epidemic caused by Christians who lack depth in understanding their identity is that they quickly begin to live outside of who they are in Christ, thus bringing shame upon the Father rather than bringing Him glory. *"In the same way, let your light shine before men, that they may see your good deeds and glorify your Father in heaven."* (Matthew 5:16)

**Sixth**, a child of the king most often has exposure to governance and decision-making. This should hopefully make sense in light of what we uncovered in our chapters on citizenship. Since we've covered this at length previously, I will use this moment to simply point out that with our identity as children of the king, we qualify for a measure of authority. However, this authority is governed by the King and only comes when one has trained and matured to the point they can steward it well. Authority is not something to play with; many lives can be destroyed by someone wielding authority carelessly.

For instance, James and John, the "sons of thunder," had just received a measure of authority from Jesus to work miracles and cast out demons. After much success on the mission field, they came back emboldened with their newly received power. On Jesus' way to Jerusalem, he found himself the recipient of rejection at the hands of Samaritans. At this, James and John asked Jesus if they should call down fire with their newfound authority to consume the Samaritans. Jesus was, of course, quick to rebuke the brothers, and I'm sure used the moment to teach the manner in which authority should be used, that is, to serve people, not to harm them.

**Seventh**, and perhaps of most importance, a king's child more easily obtains a strong sense of purpose since they are thrust into a position in which they can easily grasp the importance of their choices, since they are poised to make an impact on their region of dominance. Perhaps the greatest harm to not knowing the depths of one's identity is the lack of purpose that comes along with it. God says, *"My people are destroyed for lack of knowledge."* (Hosea 4:6) For the average citizen, discovering one's purpose may be a lifelong pursuit, and many may die having never found it. We established at the onset of this book that identity and purpose are interlocked. The truth is the average citizen and the king's child both equally have value and purpose; it's just that the king's child is born into a position that provides them with the knowledge to find their purpose, prepare for their purpose, and fulfill their purpose. Unfortunately for the average citizen, they are usually not born into such a circumstance, and they run the risk of living life stuck in cycles, unfruitful, unfulfilled, and unsatisfied. As a child of the king, we are positioned to receive purpose and preparation, and thus we have access to fruitfulness, fulfillment, and satisfaction through our Father.

Child: What is My Father Like?

## A Problem and the Solution

Yes, to be the child of a king is an exciting thing. It is a core element to the gospel truth and to what renders that truth to be "good." The child of a king inherits a unique set of advantages, and should they operate within their identity without going astray, they stand to live an enjoyable, fulfilling, and productive life. Yet, for many, this concept seems to fall short in creating a wellspring of life that flows from the inside. Shouldn't the effects of hearing this news cause a geyser to explode from the depth of our being? Yes, it should, and the fact that the well spring is dry in some is a clear indication that we have failed to teach identity in a way that is tangible and life-revolutionizing.

Now, you may be thinking that you know where I'm headed with all this. If that's you, it's likely you feel that way because you've been a Christian for some time now and have heard the phrase "I am a child of God." You likely have also been long familiar with the idea that God is a king, and therefore the concept of being a "child of the king" is not new to you. Perhaps it has even become a cliché and has an underwhelming impact on you because it falls into the category of "Christian lingo" that has no real effect on how you experience life in this fallen world. If that is you, then I invite you to hang in there with me as our journey of being a king's child is just beginning.

What you have been taught about God as our Father, Jesus our brother, and God's identity as king is all biblical and true; however, there is still a problem. Why is it that if we are taught from the foundations of Christianity our identity in Christ as sons and daughters of the king of the universe, that so many continue to live contrary to that? There are only three reasons a child of a king leaves the royal life.

**First**, a child may choose to abandon the royal life if their father is corrupt, and they wish to separate themselves from his kingdom. However, this comes with the death penalty in most cases, and thus it results in a life where the child must now live with a target on their back. Those of us who are in the kingdom have elected this path spiritually. We left the kingdom of darkness, our original abode, for His kingdom of glorious light (Colossians 1:13, 1 Peter 2:9).

**Secondly**, a child may leave their position as a child of the kingdom in the event they are led astray by lust. The little-known story of Edward VIII, the king of the United Kingdom, illustrates this. In 1936, after becoming king at the passing of his father, George V, Edward VIII abdicated the throne in order to marry Wallis Simpson. As it relates to our purposes, there is only one instance in which love would cause a king to leave their throne, and this is displayed in Christ, who left his throne and became a man to save humanity. As it pertains to Christians who fail to live out their identity as children of the King, they are most often driven away not by love, but by lust. The desires of the flesh, if untamed and left unchecked, will strip a king's child of their purpose and blind them to who they are, causing them to go down a path of self-destruction.

**Finally**, the third reason a child of the king may fail to live as such is because the child was not originally born into the family and thus, they spent a portion of their upbringing as an average citizen later to be adopted into the family. If the adopted child does not learn to transform the way they think and the way they see themselves, they will fail to adjust to their new identity and thus fail to live like the royal child they have since become. When Adam and Eve sinned, they lost their status in the kingdom, as did their children and their offspring indefinitely throughout the lanes of time. We, by default, are not children of the King; thus all twelve of the implications we spoke about above must be true of us but in the most vile and opposite ways. Without taking time to go into them all here, I invite you to take a moment and think about the five impacts a father's identity has on their children and think about the implications that it has on those who are *"...of their father the devil."*

We are not born into the kingdom. We are not even born into the family of God. Instead, we are born into iniquity. God, however, in His infinite wisdom and love for us created a solution. The first strategy God implemented, as we discussed briefly earlier, was the process of childbearing in which children are raised into godliness rather than iniquity (Malachi 2:15). However, something more potent was needed. God desired a way to restore His human family to not just godly citizens of His kingdom, but He desired that they be restored to members of His household. He desired that we might become His children once again who would eventually rule and reign with Him. For this to happen, what was previously ruined needed to be redeemed, and once redeemed, adopted.

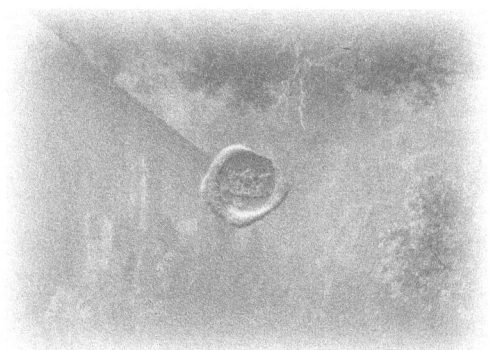

# 11. The Profound Revelation of Adoption

*For He chose us in Him before the foundation of the world to be holy and blameless in His presence. In love He predestined us for adoption as His sons through Jesus Christ, according to the good pleasure of His will.* (Ephesians 1:4-5)

"Adoption ... is the highest privilege that the gospel offers: higher even than justification." - J.I. Packer

The primary problem created at the fall of Eden is the relational disconnect between God and His image bearers. Now, instead of being born directly into the family of our Father, we are born into a different kingdom, one of iniquity that the Bible refers to as the "dominion of darkness." Paul frames the redemption story of adoption this way:

*He has rescued us from the <u>dominion of darkness</u> and brought us into the <u>kingdom of His beloved</u>*

*The* INVITATION

> *<u>Son</u>, in whom we have <u>redemption</u>, the forgiveness of sins."* (Colossians 1:13)

If you recall, we previously established that God's design for kingdom expansion is the act of childbearing. One of the core reasons God hates divorce is that it has a detrimental effect on the formation of mature children of light, thus the expansion of His kingdom. This becomes evident through God's message via Malachi the prophet:

> *It is because the LORD has been a witness between you and the wife of your youth, against whom you have broken faith, though she is your companion and your wife by covenant. Has not the LORD made them one, having a portion of the Spirit? And why one? <u>Because He seeks godly offspring.</u> So guard yourselves in your spirit and <u>do not break faith with the wife</u> of your youth.* (Malachi 2:14-15)

If childbearing was not an option, however, what could be done? This is precisely where adoption comes in. Before we look at the profound effects of being an adopted child in the coming chapter, we must first come to see the profound truths behind the act of adoption.

On September 23rd, 63 BCE, in the town of Velitrae, known today as Velletri, which is nestled on the southeast side of Rome, a child was born by the name of Gaius Octavian. Gaius was born to Gaius Octavius and Atia, who were both prominent but not necessarily important social and political figures in Rome. Gaius Octavius was a successful and wealthy Roman senator and held the office of praetor, making him part of the Roman aristocracy, though he was far from being one of the more powerful

## The Profound Revelation of Adoption

members. Atia, Octavian's mother, was of more political significance. She was the niece of Julius Caesar, which made Octavian Caesar's great-grandnephew. While this might have been an interesting fact to share with peers at dinner parties, it didn't translate to much real-life benefit. The relation to Caesar didn't come with special privilege, wealth, or power. Octavian did, however, enjoy an education appropriate to those in the families of political members. He was educated in Rome and is believed to have received an elite Roman education in rhetoric, philosophy, literature, and military tactics.

When Octavian was around four years old, he suffered the tragic loss of his father. Later, his mom would remarry Lucius Marcius Philippus, and together they would raise Octavian. After the loss of his father and as Octavian grew into his teenage years, Julius Caesar began to take an interest in Octavian. In 46 BCE, Caesar invited Octavian to join him on a military campaign in Hispania (modern-day Spain). During this trip, the young and inexperienced Octavian impressed Caesar through his zeal, courage, and ambition. Upon their return to Rome, Caesar continued to unofficially groom Octavian into a valiant leader.

While Octavian was grateful for the experience and education he received from his relationship with Caesar in Rome, he would eventually leave to study in modern-day Albania to prepare for a military campaign. In 44 BCE, at the prime age of 18, he received a gospel message that would change his life forever. While Octavian was studying abroad, Julius Caesar, the ruler that Octavian had come to love, was brutally assassinated on the Ides of March. In his despair, he was given the additional news that before his assassination, Julius Caesar had it written into his will that he officially adopted Octavian and made him the heir to the throne of Rome. The act of adoption had transformed young Octavian from a relatively obscure figure into the heir of the Roman Republic's most powerful figure. The significance of this adoption is difficult to overstate—it was as if, in a single stroke, the blood of Caesar now flowed in Octavian's veins, making him a legitimate successor to one of the most powerful legacies in the ancient world.

The road ahead would be anything but easy for Octavian. He would face a great deal of betrayal and warfare; however, he would overcome it all to make history. In 27 BCE, after years of civil war and political unrest, Octavian took on the title of Augustus, marking the end of the Roman Republic and the beginning of the Roman Empire. As Augustus Caesar, he reformed the political system, stabilized the economy, and expanded the empire's borders. His reign, known as the Pax Romana, ushered in a period of relative peace and prosperity that would last for over two centuries. Yes, I'm sure you're beginning to see now that little Octavian, one who was once relatively unknown and with no pathway to leadership, became the same Caesar we read about each Christmas season from Luke's gospel account: *"Now in those days, a decree went out from Caesar Augustus that a census should be taken of the whole empire…."* (Luke 2:1)

Isn't it a profound coincidence that the first emperor of Rome and the very emperor whose empire governed the nation of Israel at the time of Christ's birth is a living picture of exactly what Christ Jesus came to make available to each and every soul who will rely upon His name

## The Profound Revelation of Adoption

and be born again? Furthermore, we mustn't forget that it was this very system of adoption that allowed Joseph to be Jesus' legal father. That's right—Jesus was adopted by Joseph since he was not his biological father. The authors of the *Faithlife Study Bible* note in the footnotes of Matthew chapter one

> Matthew 1:16 describes Jesus' legal descent. The culture of this time considered adoption to be real sonship. Even though Jesus had no biological relation to Joseph, He continued Joseph's familial line.

I don't know about you, but I have a difficult time accepting that the timing of these historical events is fortuitous. Through Caesar Augustus' story of adoption into rulership, we get a glimpse at what Christ has made available to us who are to be adopted into the family of His Father. Furthermore, through his story, we gain an understanding of what adoption was, how it worked, what it was used for, and its lasting effects on the adopted party. There is a disconnect between adoption in the day of Paul, Christ, and Augustus and the adoption of the modern world.

In ancient Rome, the world Jesus was born into and the world the apostle Paul wrote from, adoption was not merely a private or familial decision; it was a deeply political act, imbued with far-reaching implications

> Adoption was a deeply political act, imbued with far-reaching implications for power, legacy, and identity.

for power, legacy, and identity. Unlike modern times, where adoption is often seen as a benevolent act of love and care, Roman adoption was a means of perpetuating a family's name, ensuring its wealth, influence, and social standing. It was a mechanism for legacy-building, a pathway for chosen heirs to inherit more than just assets—they inherited destinies. Julius Caesar's decision to adopt Octavian was thus not just an act of familial affection, but a political maneuver designed to secure his lineage and cement the future of Rome itself.

This single act was not just a transfer of wealth or a title—it was a transmission of *purpose*. Through the legal act of adoption, Octavian was grafted into the lineage of one of Rome's most iconic figures. He became not just a son in name, but in the public and political sense. The residents of ancient Rome and the biblical authors who wrote to us teaching on our own spiritual adoption understood that lineage was more than blood—it was about authority, legacy, and identity. Adoption was an institution that allowed individuals to transcend the circumstances of their birth and ascend to positions of authority and governance that they otherwise had no possible pathway to realizing. In the same way that Rome viewed adoption not only as a familial matter but a matter of political and "kingdom" strategy, so also God utilizes adoption as a strategy in His kingdom expansion plan.

Through Caesar Augustus' story, I am reminded of Paul's startling claim to his spiritual children in Ephesus. He writes:

> *For He <u>chose</u> us in Him before the foundation of the world to be holy and blameless in His presence.*

## The Profound Revelation of Adoption

*In love He <u>predestined us for adoption</u> as His sons <u>through Jesus Christ</u>, according to the good pleasure of His <u>will</u>.* (Ephesians 1:4-5)

It's a breathtaking reality to stop and reflect on the idea that God chose us. This verse is equivalent to the day the mail carrier showed up in Albania to reveal the news that Julius Caesar had chosen Octavian to be adopted as heir. What good news! It is for this reason I referred earlier to this news as the gospel Octavian received while studying abroad. In the same manner, Ephesians 5:1 is a letter of good news! Here we are, struggling our way through this fallen world with no hope for any sort of future. Our main objective is to get through the day while avoiding as much misery and pain as possible before dying. While living a life with no purpose, we receive a letter that tells us the God who created everything that has ever existed, both in the realms of the seen and unseen, has chosen us for adoption to rule and reign in His kingdom! This is the gospel, and it is precisely why it is referred to as "good news!"

His choice reveals to us His desire. He desires us to be adopted as His children, ones who take on the character, nature, thought processes, worldview, and desires of the Father and govern in love on the earth, which is to be the territory of God's expanding kingdom. The apostle Paul tells young Timothy that the goal of his instruction is *"the love that comes from a pure heart, clear conscience, and a sincere faith."* (1Timothy 1:5) This message aligns with his teachings to the church in Galatia, which proclaim that the most important aspect of our maturity in Christ is our *"faith working through love."* (Galatians 5:6) If Paul was at risk of being too vague in his letters to other churches, his statement to the church in Ephesus would provide explicit clarity:

> *Be imitators of God, therefore, as beloved children, and walk in love, just as Christ loved us and gave Himself up for us as a fragrant sacrificial offering to God.* (Ephesians 5:1)

To be a child is to be an imitator of one's father. In this way, when we are adopted as God's children, we begin the process of maturing into His image as intended for us in the beginning. The image of God is the living image of love which comes through our faith and spiritual maturity as we are formed by His Spirit into His likeness. Thomas Watson, a profound writer in the 17th century, wrote these words on the matter: "A man adopts one for his son and heir that does not at all resemble him; but whosoever God adopts for His child is like Him; he not only bears His heavenly Father's name, but His image."

Our adoption, though it has been accomplished, must be accepted, and we must choose to walk in it. Our adoption, our place as Children in God's kingdom, will not be forced upon us, and it is not something that simply "happens to us" involuntarily after salvation and baptism. John Chrysostom felt similarly and expressed it, saying once, "Even supposing you receive baptism, yet if you are not minded to be 'led by the Spirit' afterwards, you lose the dignity bestowed upon you, and the pre-eminence of your adoption." Yes, we are adopted by God's choice, but in order for it to become reality, we must be willing to walk in it by walking in the Spirit. That is because the Holy Spirit is our proof and evidence of adoption. When commenting on Galatians 4:5-6 which reads:

## The Profound Revelation of Adoption

*To redeem those under the law, that we might receive our adoption as sons. And because you are sons, God sent the Spirit of His Son into our hearts, crying out, "Abba, Father."*

Thomas Schreiner writes in his exegetical commentary, "The fundamental proof and evidence that the Galatians are truly God's adopted sons is that God has given them the Holy Spirit, and their sonship is expressed by their acclamation that God is their Father."

Our adoption enters into effect when we accept the invitation and rely on Christ Jesus as the Messiah who came to earth at the Father's command, lived a sinless life, and died to pay the penalty for sin. The apostle John writes:

*But to all who did receive him, he gave them the right to be children of God, to those who believe in his name, who were born, not of natural descent, or of the will of the flesh, or of the will of man, but of God.* (1 John 1:12-13)

We must receive by faith the news that has been delivered to us. What would have happened if Octavian had rejected the news of his adoption in Albania? What if he had said to himself, "This news isn't realistic; the odds of Caesar adopting me and making me heir to the republic are just not probable. No, I think I'll stay here and focus on my personal ambitions, work towards my own goals, and not waste my time with such fantasies"? The good news must either be received and accepted by faith or rejected in doubt and hardness of heart. If accepted with good soil, then we are born not of flesh but of the Spirit (John 3:6). We are born not of perishable seed but imperishable seed which leads to imperishable life as the apostle Peter proclaims, *"For you have been <u>born again</u>, not of <u>perishable</u> seed, but of <u>imperishable</u>, through the living and enduring word of God."* (1 Peter 1:23) Once we are born of the Spirit, the Spirit testifies with a resounding shout from the depths of our being that we are in fact adopted into the family of God! Again, Paul writes:

> *For you did not receive a spirit of slavery that returns you to fear, but you received the Spirit of sonship, by whom we cry, "Abba! Father!" <u>The Spirit Himself testifies with our spirit that we are God's children</u>.* (Romans 8:15)

In his 1858 sermon "The Fatherhood of God," Charles Spurgeon proclaimed, "Save heaven itself there is nought more blissful than to enjoy that spirit of adoption."

I concur that there is no greater source of joy than to remember and reflect upon our reality as adopted children into God's family. There are, however, practical implications for one who is adopted. To be adopted means one's entire world and the operation thereof will drastically change. When we read the phrase *"sons of God"* in Paul's letters (e.g., Ephesians 1:4-5), he is most often using a Greek word that is not gender-exclusive but is instead a legal term in the adoption and inheritance laws that were used in first-century Rome. This term is used to refer to those in Christ who are adopted in God's family that now and will enjoy all the privileges, obligations, and inheritance rights of God's children. In progressing forward, we must now discuss in further detail the privileges, obligations, and inheritance rights that come with our adoption into God's kingdom.

# 12. Privileges, Obligations, and Inheritances

> Under Roman law adoption secured for the adopted child a right to the name and to the property of the person by whom he had been adopted. The moment a child was adopted by a person, that child had the legal right, an absolute legal right, to make such claims. On the other hand, Roman law granted to the person who adopted the child all the rights and privileges of a father. It worked both ways. - David Martyn Lloyd-Jones (Welsh Preacher and Writer)

In the Old Testament, Israel was referred to as the son of God. The nation and people of Israel exclusively wore this status. However, God's plan to include all people in His family was seen from very early on. Tamar and Ruth are two of the gentile great-grandmothers whose line eventually led to King David. God has always provided a way for Gentiles to be incorporated into His nation and family. In the Old Testament, the way to enter God's kingdom, which was to be manifested through Israel, was a bit more rigorous. It required a laundry list of rules and regulations to be kept in order for a gentile (anyone not from the descendants of Jacob) to enter and remain a foreign resident in God's nation, Israel. In the New Testament, however, we have a new manner by which we enter His kingdom and family, that is, through receiving the gift of God's justification and reconciliation through our faith in Jesus. His kingdom now knows no bounds, and anyone, no matter their tribe or tongue, may enter. In our previous chapter, we spoke about the adoption process and how we came to be born again into the family of God. Just like with any family, the adoption into God's family comes with three major changes in the life of the adopted. Once adopted, the child receives a new set of privileges, obligations, and inheritances. Each of these is detailed throughout scripture and deserves our attention. If we neglect these, we will be like a child who has been adopted into a royal family but continues to live as a slave. It is in understanding these three categorical changes that we learn not just that we are children but how to live as children of the King.

**Privileges: Freedom**

There are a vast number of privileges we receive in our adoption as children in God's royal family. I will attempt to cover a number of them here, but I invite you to go on a treasure hunt and see how many privileges you can discover through God's Word. Here's a hint: look for the promises throughout the scriptures since every promise is a privilege we otherwise would have to live without. For the first privilege I'd like to point out, we must do a bit of Bible reading. I invite you, on your own time, to read and reflect upon a section of Paul's letter to the church in Galatia. For our purposes, I will attempt to summarize and extract the main points I wish to present. In Galatians 3:15-4:11 and verses 21-31, Paul makes a life-altering proclamation that lays out the juxtaposition between our new identity as children of God and our previous identity as *slaves to sin, the law, and the elementary principles of this world.* We are free and, as we'll discuss later, we are heirs.

The first and most fundamental privilege of life in God's family is freedom! That includes freedom in our minds, our desires, and our emotions. It includes freedom from the law which binds and from the kingdom of darkness which leads to death. Jesus came to set the captives free, and that freedom is the transition from a prison cell located in a dark, wet, fringed dungeon into the abundant life of marvelous light, which is in the Son, Christ Jesus. Jesus proclaimed these prophetic words when describing why the Father sent Him to the earth:

> *The Spirit of the Lord is on Me, because He has anointed Me to preach good news to the poor. <u>He has sent Me to proclaim liberty to the captives</u> and recovery of sight to the blind, to release the oppressed, to proclaim the year of the Lord's favor.* (Luke 4:18-19)

In Christ, you are free from that which has previously bound you. However, this freedom must be something you choose to walk in, refusing to return to your previous ways before being in Christ. It is for this very reason the apostle Paul implores us to "stay free." "So, Christ has truly set us free. Now *make sure that you stay free*, and don't get tied up again in slavery to the law." (Galatians 5:1) It is for this reason I strongly encourage you to seek out a biblically sound pastoral counselor or spiritual director who is equipped to help you live a life of Christlikeness through the ongoing processes of discipleship. This form of counseling is often undervalued because it is not something that requires a state license. However, good one-on-one discipleship and godly counseling are worth more than a thousand sessions with a secular psychotherapist.

**Privileges: A Father's Love**

I would be remiss if I did not take time to talk about one of the greatest, if not the greatest, epidemic among Christians today, and that is the lack of revelation surrounding God's unique and extravagant love towards them. I place this in the privilege category because, in my opinion, it is a privilege to be loved when we were yet His enemies (Romans 5:8). We live in a land inundated with misconceptions about God and His Fatherly love towards us. Misconceptions of God's fatherly love are often shaped by negative experiences with our own earthly fathers, misunderstandings of biblical teachings, or unhealthy cultural influences. If we wish to experience the fullness of His love and to live from that identity, we must deal with these misconceptions.

## Privileges, Obligations, and Inheritances

Now, another short book could be penned focusing just on all the misconceptions we have and the truth that must be replaced, because the enemy has been hard at work creating false ideas and deceptions to keep God's children from receiving and walking in His love. At our counseling ministry Whole Soul Counsel, we spend the vast majority of time working through these misconceptions during our spiritual care and counseling sessions. Since I won't have time to unpack them all here, I again invite you to seek godly counsel and spiritual direction.

Among the most popular misconceptions are lies such as "God's love is conditional or must be earned," "God is distant or uninvolved," "God is punitive and harsh," "God is impersonal and unrelatable," "God is disappointed in me," "God's love must be the same as human love," "God is more concerned with rules than relationship," or "God hasn't forgiven me fully." I wish I could address them all here because what I have come to learn about being human is that no one is exempt from thoughts and emotions that would tempt us to believe any number of these lies to be reality. In brief, I'd like to say that God's love for you is not like that of your earthly father's love. He cannot be compared or likened to human love; He is infinitely better. God is not absent or uninvolved even if you've encountered a life full of people who have abandoned you and, as a result, crippled your self-worth; God is the *ever-present* help in time of need. He promised to *never leave nor forsake us*! God is not disappointed in you—if He was, then He wouldn't

> God's love for you is not like that of your earthly father's love.

have sent His Son to die on the cross, for He foreknew you and all your mistakes from the beginning of time, yet He loved you enough to send Jesus 2,000 years before you were conceived, and He loves you just the same today despite the mistakes you've made and will inevitably make in the future. You have immense worth in Christ! The potential reality of having a relationship with you is what gave Jesus the strength to endure the cross. He told us that it was *"joy set before Him"* that enabled Him to endure the cross. You were the joy set before Him; therefore, never let the enemy discredit your worth.

**Privilege: Security, Protection, and Provision**

Finally, as children in God's kingdom, we receive security, protection, and provision.

When Jesus taught His disciples to pray, he said *"...give us this day our daily bread...forgive us our trespasses... lead us not into temptation but deliver us from evil."* (Matthew 6:9-13) In this short prayer, we see that eternal security through the forgiveness of our sins is available to us in addition to protection from evil and the meeting of our bodily needs. In a royal setting, the children are secure financially and in their purpose. They have no fear of losing their status nor of experiencing lack. They are equipped with royal guards for protection, and they live in security behind the hedges and walls of their Father's kingdom. In the same way, we enjoy safety and security as children of God. In His famous sermon on the mount, Jesus dedicates a moment to addressing anxiety and fear. He teaches that we ought not to worry about what we will eat, drink, or wear since the Father feeds the birds and clothes the flowers of the fields. If He cares for the birds and the grass of the earth, how much more His children? Jesus declared, *"Don't worry about these things for your Father knows you need them. Instead seek the Kingdom and its righteousness and all these things will be added to you."* (Matthew 6:32 paraphrased) In other words, the solution to your fear is to remember who you belong to and to seek the Kingdom and its righteousness, since as a child of God your needs will be met both in this life and in eternity.

**Obligations: Imitate and Expand.**

In a family system, each member has a role and responsibility. These responsibilities are not optional; in other words, if they go undone there are consequences. Therefore, these roles are obligations, but we must be explicitly clear about this term. By obligation, we do not mean to suggest that one must "earn their keep" or that if one fails to fulfill their roles or responsibilities, their adoption is somehow revoked. This isn't to be treated like employment because families operate differently than corporations.

Growing up, I can remember each Christmas and Thanksgiving when our family and extended family would gather to celebrate with big meals and festive activities; each member of the family volunteered for or was assigned tasks appropriate to their age, maturity, and skills. Some may have the role of cooking the turkey, others may carve the turkey, while others may take out the trash—as a young pup, that was usually my job. Everyone had an obligation to contribute and to play a specific role in the sustaining and expansion of the family. The same applies to us as children in the family of God. For this reason, we are given gifts, and as we mature, authority for the purpose of sustaining and expanding our kingdom on the earth.

The premier obligation we have as children in the kingdom is to be an imitator of our Father as image bearers and representatives on the earth. In the ancient world, the title "children of" or "child" was a metaphoric vernacular for describing someone who is an imitator of their father. Paul writes to his church in Ephesus:

> *Be imitators of God, therefore, as beloved children, and walk in love, just as Christ loved us and gave Himself up for us as a fragrant sacrificial offering to God.* (Ephesians 5:1-2)

Notice he says to be imitators—as children. Therefore, to be a child of God first and foremost is a means of suggesting that we know God's character and nature and we imitate that with our lives. I once heard pastor Bill Johnson of Bethel church say, "To represent Jesus is to re-present Jesus." That is the essence of childhood in the biblical vernacular. We can see another illustration beautifully in the gospel of John Chapter 8. Jesus is in the midst of a dispute with the Pharisees when they begin to shift into the "child-father" vernacular. The narrative reads:

> *"Abraham is our father," they replied. "If you were children of Abraham," said Jesus, "you would do the works of Abraham. But now you are trying to kill Me, a man who has told you the truth that I heard from God. Abraham never did such a thing. You are doing the works of your father (the devil)."* (John 8:39-41)

As children of the Father, we are to do the works of the Father. This is, of course, what is meant by imitating. In order to do the Father's works, we must first become like our Father. This happens through our partnership with the Holy Spirit as we are sanctified and made more like Christ. The apostle Peter teaches that we are sanctified, that is, to be made into Christlikeness by the Holy Spirit for the purpose of obedience: *"...and sanctified by the Spirit for obedience to Jesus Christ."* (1 Peter 1:2) In the narrative we looked at briefly from John chapter 8, Jesus ties obedience to imitating. In other words, the father of both the kingdom of light and darkness commands us to be like them on the earth, and depending on who we are imitating is who we are obeying.

Make no mistake about it, the Holy Spirit is the agent of our transformation, we are partners and mustn't sit idly by hoping it just happens involuntarily. Paul explicitly tells Timothy that:

> *If anyone cleanses himself of what is unfit, he will be a vessel for honor: sanctified, useful to the Master, and prepared for every good work.* (2 Timothy 2:21)

The apostle John affirms this idea by teaching, *"And everyone who has this hope in Him purifies himself, just as Christ is pure."* (1 John 3:3) We must seek and pursue God's nature and love to be deposited into us, and then we must obey when the Spirit prompts us through the subtle nudge of conviction. As we seek Him, He will give us new thoughts and desires in line with His (Psalm 37:4), but it is up to us to utilize our will to walk them out when prompted. In this way, we partner with God in expanding His kingdom as His imagers on the earth, and we partner in our own sanctification process of Christ being formed in us.

## Inheritance: Heirs and Co-heirs

As children of God, we will receive, in due time, our inheritance. Though it is true and wonderful news that we have an inheritance, it is not the primary message taught in scripture. In other words, it is present but not the focus. There is greater attention placed upon the reality that we, the body of believers, the adopted family of God, are first His inheritance. It is critical that we understand what this means and how it relates to our identity; therefore, we will give more attention to it in the final section of this book. For now, however, it is important that we understand our inheritance so that we will live as those who are looking ahead to a future glory.

Paul writes in his letters to the Romans this fundamental truth regarding our identity as children of God:

> *The Spirit Himself testifies with our spirit that <u>we are God's children</u>. And if we are children, then we are heirs: <u>heirs of God</u> and <u>co-heirs with Christ</u>—if indeed we suffer with Him, so that we may also be glorified with Him.* (Romans 8:17)

When the Bible teaches that we are Heirs of God, it refers to being granted access into God's family and, as a result, access to all that is His and of Him. We are heirs to the kingdom and its realities. We are heirs to eternal life, complete sanctification, and a renewed and perfected spirit that is once again in union with the Father as it was prior to the fall in Eden.

As co-heirs with Christ, we will rule and reign with Him in His kingdom. The apostle John wrote about the saints in Revelation:

> *Nevertheless, hold fast to what you have until I come. And to the one who overcomes and continues in My work until the end, I will give authority over the nations."* (Revelation 2:25-26)

He further adds, *"You have made them to be a kingdom and priests to serve our God, and <u>they will reign upon the earth</u>."* (Revelation 5:10) As you read your Bible, you will see the apostles most often verify each other through their letters. Paul writes to Timothy and confirms what John wrote in his revelatory account. He says, *"If we endure, <u>we will also reign with Him</u>; if we deny Him, He will also deny us...."* (2 Timothy 2:12)

## Inheritance: Glorification and Rewards

To conclude this section, I must include that as children of God, we will also inherit the glorification of our bodies; that is, we will receive resurrected bodies which will never die nor decay. Furthermore, all of creation will be restored and be outside of the curse of death. Again, in his letter to the Romans, Paul writes:

> *The creation waits in eager expectation for the revelation of the sons of God. For <u>the creation was subjected to futility</u>, not by its own will, but because of the One who subjected it, in the hope that the <u>creation itself will be set free from its bondage to decay</u> and brought into the glorious freedom of the children of God.* (Romans 8:19-21)

Finally, we as children will receive rewards; however, this particular inheritance is subject to vary per believer in accordance with how we stewarded the life we have on earth. Jesus was explicit about the judgment in John's vision. He said:

> *And I saw the dead, great and small, standing before the throne. And there were open books, and one of them was the Book of Life. And <u>the dead were judged according to their deeds</u>, as recorded in the books.* (Revelation 20:12)

Elsewhere He proclaimed, *"For the Son of Man will come in His Father's glory with His angels, and then He will repay each one according to what he has done."* (Matthew 16:27)

Therefore, let us make every aim to grow in and walk in our identity as children, disciples, citizens, and His inheritance.

# About the Author

K. Lee Brown is a pastor, counselor, and writer whose life's work centers on helping others live with a whole soul in a broken world. Through teaching biblical truth and guiding others into the way of Jesus, he invites readers to step into the transformative journey of becoming a new creation.

A devoted husband and father, Lee finds deep meaning in the life he shares with his wife and two children. His work spans poetry, nonfiction, and children's tales—each crafted with a heart to illuminate the beauty of living from the Kingdom of God here and now, and to foster emotional and spiritual health along the way.

You can access an abundance of Lee's free content via www.KLBrown.org

Scan the QR code for a free Study Guide!

or visit:

https://www.truepotentialmedia.com/invitation/

www.ingramcontent.com/pod-product-compliance
Lightning Source LLC
Chambersburg PA
CBHW031259110426
42743CB00041B/749